DISABLED PEOPLE AND EUROPEAN HUMAN RIGHTS

A review of the implications of
the 1998 Human Rights Act for
disabled children and adults in the UK

Luke Clements and Janet Read

The POLICY

P~P

PRESS

First published in Great Britain in February 2003 by

The Policy Press
34 Tyndall's Park Road
Bristol BS8 1PY
UK

Tel: +44 (0)117 954 6800
Fax: +44 (0)117 973 7308
Email: tpp@bristol.ac.uk
www.policypress.org.uk

British Library Cataloguing in Publication Data

A catalogue record for this book is available from the British Library

ISBN 1 86134 425 2

Luke Clements is Senior Research Fellow at Cardiff Law School and **Janet Read** is Senior Lecturer in the School of Health and Social Studies, University of Warwick.

Cover design by Qube Design Associates, Bristol.
Printed and bound in Great Britain by Bell & Bain Ltd, Glasgow.

Contents

Acknowledgements

We especially thank Chiade O'Shea, Brian McGinnis, Camilla Parker, Jenny McGhie and John Harris for their help in writing this book.

Abbreviations of law reports

AC	Appeal Court Reports
Admin LR	Administrative Law Review
All ER	All England Law Reports
BML	Butterworths Medical Law Reports
CA	Court of Appeal
CCLR	Community Care Law Reports
Crim LR	Criminal Law Review
DLR	Dominion Law Reports
DR	Decisions and Reports
East	East's Term reports, English Law Reports Vols 102-104
ECJ	European Court of Justice
EHRR	European Human Rights Reports
EWCA	England and Wales Court of Appeal (Neutral Citation)
Fam	Family Reports
Fam Law	Family Law
FCR	Family Court Reports
FLR	Family Law Reports
HRLR	Human Rights Law Reports
NZLR	New Zealand Law Reports
PD	Law Reports Probate Division
QBD	Queen's Bench Division Reports
SCC	Supreme Court Cases (India)
SCJ	Supreme Court Journal (India)
SLT	Scots Law Times
UKHRR	UK Human Rights Reports
US	United States Supreme Court Reports
WLR	Weekly Law Reports

Table of cases

Note: A note number is given in brackets after the page number when a case is referred to in the text without being cited, the citation appearing in the notes at the end of the chapter.

Table of legislation

Introduction

Much of the literature that seeks to describe the experiences of disabled people using the language of human rights has been written by non-lawyers. This literature has proved to be of enormous importance, since it has enabled the development of discourses which explore the whole spectrum of disabled people's experiences, untrammelled by the constraints of the legalistic approach. Human rights cannot ultimately be defined by or confined to International Conventions and Covenants. While these documents are within the province of the law, they usually reflect and condense prevalent philosophies of rights developed, for the most part, by non-lawyers.

The dearth of legal texts[1] in this field however, has been the subject of comment. Hendriks (1999, p 113) for example, refers to the silence of human rights scholars, and Gostin and Mann (1999, p 54) comment upon a similar absence in the field of health and human rights. It is hoped that in considering the implications of the Human Rights Act for disabled people, this book will, in addition to analysing the reasons for this relative silence, make a small contribution towards redressing the balance.

On one level, the lack of legal comment on disabled people's human rights has a relatively straightforward explanation. Until recently, with the exception of the field of mental health detention, there have been remarkably few human rights cases litigated in international and domestic tribunals that are of direct relevance to disabled people. Case law is the raw material for most legal commentaries and without it there is only a limited amount that can be said. Such an explanation however, begs the inevitable question as to why there have been so few cases. We suggest the answer does not lie in the fact that Human Rights Conventions are not directly relevant to the experiences of disabled people, but in the problem of access. Simply, that disabled people have been severely handicapped by the legal process in accessing these rights. In many respects, the problem is not so much with the rights as with the lack of access to effective remedies. Without significant procedural reform, it is likely that, for most disabled people, these rights will remain illusory and hypothetical. We regard this to be one of the central themes of the book.

Frustrating for non-lawyers as the silence of legal human rights scholars may have been, it is at times equally frustrating for lawyers to see important articles on human rights and disability overlook relevant judgments, or (at best) relegate them to an inconclusive footnote. A major aim of this book, therefore, is to take stock and to bring into the domain of social policy and social theory on disability, an analysis of the increasing body of court and tribunal decisions that may have a direct bearing on the human rights of disabled people.

By giving a primary focus to the output of the legal process, we have inevitably had to quote from judgments and other legal texts in which the use of language is frequently at variance with that used by many disabled people. Two important points arise from this difference in the nature of expression. The first concerns the continued use by judges and legal texts of phrases no longer considered appropriate by many disabled people, such as 'mentally handicapped' or 'retarded'. While this may be indicative of the perspectives and prejudices of many judges and lawmakers, it is nevertheless a fact that we have had to accept, in order to be able to quote faithfully from these primary sources. The second issue is more subtle. One consequence of the law's historically marginal role for disabled people has been that disability campaigners and commentators have created a particular human rights language to describe the oppression experienced by disabled people. While this language shares many similar principles, words and constructions with that of the language of human rights used by the law, it nevertheless remains distinct from it. Accordingly phrases, such as 'degrading treatment' do not always read across. The depth and complexity of this concept as appreciated by a disabled person, is not fully reflected in the essentially restrictive definition adopted by the courts. The latter may appear rather two-dimensional to the disabled person who believes that they have experienced what it is to be truly degraded. Nevertheless the law can be a powerful and flexible tool that is capable not only of articulating many of the injustices experienced by disabled people, but also of combating them.

In this book, we have deliberately concentrated our analysis on those areas of human rights and disability that have previously received little legal attention. The focus will be on the human rights of people living with physical and sensory impairment and learning disability. While reference will be made on occasion, to people who experience mental health difficulties, in the main this will be to draw on legal decisions which may also have a bearing on those disabled people who are the main subjects of this book. Fortunately, human rights in relation to mental health is one area that has already attracted substantial legal comment.

In addition, we are mainly concerned with the present state of the law and do not therefore consider in detail the likely impact of, as yet unimplemented, provisions such as the disability discrimination provisions within the Treaty of Amsterdam[2], or Protocol 12 of the European Convention on Human Rights[3].

The book is comprised of five chapters. In order to contextualise the application of the European Convention on Human Rights and the 1998 Human Rights Act, the first chapter gives an account of major policy and legislative changes affecting disabled people in the United Kingdom in the post-Second World War period. Chapter 2 provides a review of the European Convention on Human Rights and the 1998 Human Rights Act. Chapter 3 draws on research and other literature to analyse key human rights issues identified as significant to disabled children and adults in the United Kingdom. Chapter 4 considers how the Human Rights Act may impact on the human rights issues that have been regarded as important for disabled people. The final chapter debates the barriers and opportunities for the practical application of the Human Rights Act for the benefit of disabled people in the United Kingdom.

Notes

[1] A notable and early exception being Daw, 2000.

[2] Which amends the EC Treaty (Article 13 EC) to enable the EU to take appropriate action to combat discrimination based on (among other things) disability. For a review of its potential impact, see for instance Whittle (2000) and Flynn (1999).

[3] Which widens the scope of the non-discrimination provision in Article 14, see Chapter 3.

ONE

Social policy and disabled people: a recent history

Introduction

This chapter provides an overview of major legislative and policy developments affecting disabled people in the UK in the half century following the end of the Second World War, a period coterminus with that following the ratification of the European Convention on Human Rights (the Convention) by the UK.

There are a number of reasons for providing such an overview. First, both the European Convention and the 1998 Human Rights Act (HRA) have to be understood in relation to the policy and legislative contexts in which they are to be applied. They intersect with existing legislation. In addition, as will be outlined in Chapter 2, a core dimension of both the Convention and the HRA concerns the obligations of public bodies to individual citizens. This makes it important to understand the nature of state action and inaction in relation to disabled children and adults over this period. Any exploration of this kind reveals, among other things, the ways in which the disabled person's relationship with the state has been characterised by a combination of essential provision conjoined with oppression and violation of their human rights. Another and important dimension for any contextualising analysis of the type envisaged in this chapter concerns the various forces that have challenged the status quo and promoted change. In the late 20th century, the Disabled People's Movement proved to be one such force and its impact is discussed at the end of the chapter.

In Chapter 2 we discuss how in the context of international conventions and covenants, human rights may be grouped into two categories: civil and political on the one hand and economic, social and cultural on the other. In this chapter, therefore, we aim to lay the groundwork for the socio-legal discussions that follow, by grouping the policy and legislative developments of the post-war period within the same categories.

Civil and political rights embrace what are sometimes known as 'negative' or 'hard' rights. Essentially the defining characteristic of such rights is that they are concerned with acts that the state should refrain from doing. Examples include the right not to be subjected to torture or abuse, discrimination, arbitrary imprisonment or unreasonable state interference with one's family or private life. On the other hand, economic, social and cultural rights, are often known as 'positive' or 'soft' rights since they place an obligation on the state positively to do something, for instance, to provide health and education services, social security and employment and so on. While such categories are helpful in some respects, a neat delineation between these rights is not of course, always possible.

Civil and political rights

Because of their vital and overarching relevance to the lives of all people we begin with a brief overview of policy and legislation related to the civil and political rights of disabled people.

The protection of life, abuse, forced treatment and detention

Although the right to life constitutes the most fundamental of human rights, its protection has not been unequivocal for disabled people in the post-war period. Across this period, the debate about whether disabled people have the right to life on the same basis as their non-disabled peers, has emerged and re-emerged at various times and in various forms. The debate has in particular questioned whether there are circumstances that permit parents and/or doctors and/or the courts to take a decision that a young disabled child, often a baby, should not survive (Shearer, 1984).

The case of Baby Alexandra in 1980 and the trial of Dr Leonard Arthur in 1981, are two of the British examples on which a great deal of public and professional attention has been focused. In the former, a local authority applied for a child with Down's syndrome to be made a ward of the court after her parents had refused to give consent to life-saving surgery. One hospital had attempted to protect the child and ensure that she had the treatment by alerting the local authority. However, when she was subsequently transferred to another hospital for surgery, the surgeon declined to operate having heard the parents' wishes. The local authority was eventually successful and the child survived. In the second case, a consultant paediatrician was charged with murder, (later reduced to attempted murder) and acquitted after having prescribed sedation and nursing care only for a baby with Down's Syndrome whose parents did not wish him to survive. The procedure inevitably resulted in the child's death.

To regard these cases simply as isolated acts by individuals is to misunderstand the context entirely for there is no doubt that they were representative of practice in public organisations that was by no means unusual. Papers in the professional journals of the period indicate at least three significant issues as far as disabled people's human rights are concerned (Wolfensberger, 1980; Johnson, 1981; Kuhse, 1984; Shearer, 1984; Fairbairn, 1988; Raphael, 1988). First, the practice of ensuring that some disabled babies did not survive was fairly widespread. Secondly, by no means everyone in the relevant professions regarded disabled children as having an equal right to life on a par with their non-disabled peers. Consequently, some saw a procedure to bring about their deaths as justifiable. One of the determining factors which influenced the decision-making by the professionals involved, was a judgment about the projected quality of life that the disabled person was seen to be likely to have. Thirdly, on occasions, terms with passive connotations such as 'allowing to die' obscured practices which were designed to bring about death.

Later in the 20th century, the law and legal decisions became clearer in this regard. One feature of the 1989 Children Act was that it set out to bring disabled children within the legislative framework designed to offer protection and support equally to all children who needed it. As we shall consider further in Chapter 3, it is the current and emphatic approach taken by the courts that it is not within their prerogative "to look down upon a disadvantaged person and judge the quality of that person's life to be so low as not to be deserving of continuance"[1]. This, of course is not the statutory position as it applies to foetuses. Section 1 of the 1967 Abortion Act, in effect, legalised abortions where "there is a substantial risk that if the child were born it would suffer from such physical or mental abnormalities as to be seriously handicapped".

There have also been on-going debates in the media and professional literature about the extent to which disabled people are given access to the healthcare treatment they need on an equal basis to those who are non-disabled (BBC, 1998; Morris, 1999b). The issue of whether discriminatory attitudes by doctors to children with Down's syndrome might have affected the treatment they received formed part of the independent inquiries into paediatric cardiac services at two London hospitals (Evans Report, 2001).

With the exception of the 1967 Abortion Act (itself a Private Member's Bill) and the 1983 Mental Health Act, legislative involvement in relation to both medical interventions and the abuse of disabled people can be characterised by its absence: Parliament essentially relying upon an ad hoc development of the common law by the judiciary. The severe problems caused by the inadequate state of the law in this field were addressed by the Law Commission, which in 1995 published its seminal report *Mental incapacity*[2]. A draft Mental Incapacity Bill annexed to the report sought to clarify the meaning in law of mental incapacity and to regulate its consequences in three key areas: medical treatment decisions, substitute decision-making in relation to matters of finance and personal welfare, and protection from significant harm or serious exploitation. Despite compelling arguments that all of these issues require urgent legislative attention, none has been forthcoming. In relation to concerns about the widespread physical, financial and sexual abuse of disabled adults, the most tangible response has been the policy guidance publications: in England, *No secrets*[3] (DoH and the Home Office, 2000), and in Wales *In safe hands*[4] (National Assembly for Wales, 2000). We suggest in Chapter 3, that as yet these may have made very little impact in the level of abuse experienced by disabled people.

The energetic prosecution of people who ill-treat disabled people is an essential element in any system that professes to uphold respect for their personal integrity. Again, there was, until recently, little evidence that this obligation was being addressed in the UK and considerable evidence to suggest that the treatment of disabled victims of crime was deplorable (Sanders, 1997). Part of this problem has been the reluctance of the judiciary to accept as probative, the evidence of many victims of crime with learning difficulties. In this respect at least significant improvements have now been effected via Part II of the 1999 Youth Justice and Criminal Evidence Act, which is intended to ensure that as many people as possible are able to give evidence at trial (Birch, 2000).

In relation to the detention of disabled people, 1948 saw the enactment of Section 47 of the National Assistance Act authorising the removal from their homes of certain chronically sick, disabled or elderly persons (a power provided primarily to facilitate slum clearance rather than for any humanitarian purpose; see Gray, 1979). Although, as we discuss in Chapter 3, serious questions arise concerning its compatibility with the Convention, it remains on the statute book.

Of far greater importance, however, was the 1959 Mental Health Act. The Act codified the disparate 'lunacy' and 'asylum' laws of the previous 100 years and introduced many of the safeguards and procedures present in the current legislation. These included the principle that no one should be admitted to hospital if care in the community would be more appropriate, and that where admission to hospital was required, compulsion should, if possible, be avoided (Jones, 1999). The 1959 Act was substantially amended by the 1982 Mental Health (Amendment) Act to reflect changes in treatment, care regimes and important decisions of the European Court of Human Rights (considered in Chapter 3), and then was largely repealed by the codifying enactment of the 1983 Mental Health Act.

Notwithstanding the procedural safeguards in the 1983 Act, the fact remains that today, as discussed in Chapter 3, the vast majority of disabled people who are de facto detained in psychiatric wards and care homes are kept there informally and without any legal protection. The enactment of the 1998 HRA has brought this situation (now commonly referred to as the Bournewood gap) to the fore and, as we also suggest later, a legislative response is now inevitable.

Personal integrity, private and sexual rights and property

The last 50 years have seen considerable changes to social mores on sexual conduct, and this too has been reflected in legislative change. The law in relation to gay and lesbian rights provides one such example. Some of the changes have been influenced by what might be regarded as progressive decisions of the European Court of Human Rights in Strasbourg (here referred to as the Court). There has, however, been no significant legislative reform concerning the rights of disabled people to a sexual life. As the Home Office Consultation Paper 'Setting the Boundaries: Reforming the law on sex offences' (Home Office, 2000) noted[5]: "current legislation [the 1956 Sexual Offences Act] proscribes all sexual activity with those with severe learning disabilities – such absolute proscription of all sexual activity, may constitute a breach of Article 8, which guarantees a right to respect for private and family life".

In 2000[6], the Law Commission had stressed that any review of the law required the striking of an "appropriate balance between paternalism and the right to respect for private life" and strongly implied that legislative rebalancing was necessary.

The battle for anti-discrimination legislation

Across the 1980s and 1990s an increasingly active and well-organised Disabled People's Movement focused its efforts on identifying the oppression experienced by disabled people and on winning civil rights and equal opportunities (Abberley, 1987; Barnes, 1990; Bynoe et al, 1991; Morris, 1991; Campbell and Oliver, 1996). The introduction of anti-discrimination legislation was seen to be a crucial element in the broader struggle for disabled people's rights.

Throughout this period, a number of Private Member's Bills were introduced in the face of a government emphatic that education and persuasion, rather than legislation, represented the appropriate way to pursue equal opportunities for disabled people (Doyle, 1997). There was a substantial outcry in 1994, when the Civil Rights (Disabled Persons) Bill, another Private Member's Bill, was defeated by the government employing parliamentary procedure to block it. A weakened administration responded both to initial and sustained pressure by introducing its own Bill in 1995, and amending it throughout its passage through parliament (Doyle, 1997). The Disability Discrimination Act (DDA) received royal assent later the same year.

The DDA made it unlawful to discriminate against disabled people in connection with employment, the provision of goods, facilities and services or the disposal and management of premises. It also contained measures related to increasing accessibility of public transport. The provisions were to be implemented across a period ending in 2004.

The Act was widely seen by disabled people and their organisations as weak and disappointing. While recognising its limitations, however, some saw it as a small milestone, a first statement of its kind and a tool that it might be possible to use for the benefit of disabled people. Others commented that it could be construed as an indication that headway had been made in establishing the extent to which disabled people's opportunities were restricted by factors extrinsic to their physical and intellectual abilities (Drake, 1999).

One of the major reservations about the DDA was that it did not establish a Commission for disability rights comparable to those safeguarding the interests of women and minority ethnic groups. The Labour Party, returned to office in 1997, had pledged to remedy this and did so via the 1999 Disability Rights Commission Act, with the Commission coming into being in 2000.

Economic, social and cultural rights

We turn now to an overview of policy and legislative initiatives in the post-war period which can be encompassed within the category of 'positive' or 'soft' rights.

Income maintenance and employment

The Beveridge Report (1942) and the legislation that followed in its wake, established both the principles and the provision which lay at the centre of the post-war Welfare State. While introducing a range of new measures, Beveridge also rationalised and extended provisions which had been growing in a piecemeal fashion throughout the first half of the 20th century. Disabled people benefited from some provisions which were available to the general population together with other measures designed specifically with them in mind.

A major principle underpinning the Beveridge social security reforms was that poverty resulted from interruptions to employment, through for instance, pregnancy, sickness, injury or retirement. Accordingly, the scheme was insurance based. Individuals made contributions from their income while earning in order to establish a right to benefits when sick or unemployed. The ability to benefit, therefore, rested on access and fitness to work. An additional principle was that of compensation. Compensatory benefits in the form of war pensions and those for industrial injury had grown incrementally in the first half of the 20th century. For those without the necessary contributions, or who were not entitled to compensation, means-tested benefits designed to be at subsistence level were established (Drake, 1999).

In order to increase work opportunities for disabled people, special measures, including the 1944 Disabled Persons (Employment) Act were introduced. The Act contained various provisions including employment rehabilitation, training, sheltered employment for disabled people, and an obligation upon larger employers that disabled people (drawn from the registers of disabled people) should make up at least 3% of their workforce. The Act was unenforced and largely ignored and albeit, not formally repealed until 1995 (Drake, 1999). As we shall discuss in Chapter 3, research has consistently indicated that economically active disabled people face significant barriers in relation to employment, a disadvantaged position that cannot be explained wholly in terms of their functional abilities (Walker, 1982; Lonsdale, 1990; Anderson, 1995; Barnes et al, 1998).

The effect of the post-war Beveridge reforms was that those disabled people who had never had access to work, or who had not become disabled as a consequence of war or industrial injury, were seriously disadvantaged financially. These included women who were married or caring for their families and individuals disabled from childhood. Until the mid-1970s, there were no cash benefits paid as of right to them. In addition, the existing benefits had never been set at the level regarded as adequate by Beveridge, such that by the mid-

1970s the income maintenance benefits available to the British disabled person, expressed as a percentage of wages, were lower than any other country in the European Community (Topliss, 1975).

In the 1970s, official recognition of the disadvantaged position of those unable to build a contributions record and of the high costs of disabled living, resulted in the introduction of a number of non-contributory benefits such as Attendance Allowance, Non-contributory Invalidity Pension, Invalid Care Allowance and Mobility Allowance. In 1991 the Disability Living Allowance and Disability Working Allowance were introduced in an attempt to support disabled people entering and remaining in employment without losing out financially.

Despite these reforms, disabled people and those close to them, continue to have insufficient income to offset the combined impact of the additional costs of disabled living and the restricted opportunities to generate income (Bertoud et al, 1993; Dobson and Middleton, 1998; Drake, 1999).

Local authority and health services

The 1948 National Assistance Act enabled (and in some cases required) local authorities to make various forms of assistance available to disabled people, including accommodation. Until 1970, it remained the main piece of legislation covering local authority responsibilities to disabled people. There was enormous variation from one area to another in terms of the types and availability of services provided under the 1948 Act by the local authority welfare departments. Where services existed, they were frequently at a minimal level and came in the form of restrictive and frequently unacceptable options (Simkins and Tickner, 1978; Campbell and Oliver, 1996). The accommodation provided under Part III of the Act was usually restricted to care in residential institutions, some of which were under the auspices of charities. It was not until 1970, that local authorities were given duties in relation to the adaptation and provision of housing for disabled people.

Across the second half of the 20th century, a gradual shift can be seen in the balance of responsibilities between the health service and local authorities. In the thirty years following the war, the health services, including the public health departments of local authorities, played a major role in relation to disabled children and adults. For example, decisions about disabled children's schooling relied heavily on medical diagnosis and recommendation (Sutton, 1982), and prior to the coming into force of the 1970 Education (Handicapped Children) Act, the public health departments were responsible for the junior training centres for those children with learning disabilities deemed to be ineducable.

The last 50 years, however, has seen a steady decline in the role of the NHS as an institutional accommodater of disabled people. At its inception in 1946 it became responsible for the long stay subnormality [sic] hospitals, regarded at this time as the standard provision for many people with learning disabilities. Large numbers of adults and children spent long periods of their lives in such establishments, and in the late 1960s and early 1970s a number of research and official reports drew attention to the depriving conditions that were all too prevalent (for example, DHSS, 1969; Oswin, 1971).

In 1970, following the publication of the Seebohm report (Seebohm, 1968) and the enactment of the 1970 Local Authority Social Services Act, the children's and mental health services, together with those provided by the welfare departments for disabled and older adults, were made the responsibility of new unified local authority social services departments. Short- and long-term hospital-based provision for people with learning disabilities was also to be transferred to local authorities (DHSS, 1971). The formation of the new social services departments marked an expansion in the influence of professional social work which was seen to be the core of their operations.

In 1970 also came the introduction of one of the most significant pieces of legislation for disabled people in the post-war period, the Chronically Sick and Disabled Persons Act. Contemporary commentators (Topliss, 1978) suggest that the data from the OPCS survey on disabled people (Harris, 1971), circulated in advance of its publication, provided a major impetus for the introduction of this legislation. The survey revealed three million disabled people in private households, many of whom were receiving little, if any, assistance despite high levels of need. Many were entirely unknown to any of the agencies with responsibilities towards them.

The Act was complex and wide-ranging, requiring the involvement of eleven ministries and the amendment of 39 existing acts of parliament (Simkins and Tickner, 1978). It required local authorities to ascertain the numbers of disabled people in their areas and to publish information about services for them. New public buildings were required to be accessible to disabled people. Local authorities in the form of the new social services departments, were empowered under Section 2 of the Act to provide a range of services designed to support disabled people living in their own homes. These included the provision of practical assistance in the home, radio, television and library facilities, recreational and educational facilities, travel, structural adaptations to the home, equipment, holidays, meals and telephones.

While it was hailed by many at the time as the disabled person's charter and while it has remained the cornerstone of community care provision to the present day, the Act failed to have the impact on the lives of disabled people that some had hoped. There were a number of reasons for this. First, some contemporary commentators argued that despite good intentions, the Act was fundamentally flawed in that it shifted the emphasis towards discretionary services and provisions in kind, rather than focusing on policies to ensure that disabled people had an adequate income and the chance to choose and purchase for themselves the things that they needed (Simkins and Tickner, 1978; Toplis, 1978; Shearer, 1982). This reliance on local authority services drew disabled people into a dependent relationship with the personal social services which many have argued both at the time, and subsequently, to be unwarranted and damaging (Simkins and Tickner, 1978; Morris, 1993). It also has to be remembered that whatever the responsibilities of the new social services departments, social work and social work training at this point in its history, placed little emphasis either on the needs of disabled people or on practical and material problems faced by service users more generally (Bond, 1971; Oliver, 1983; CCETSW, 1987; Read, 1987a, b). In addition, no sooner was the Act on the statute book, than it fell foul of the repercussions on Western economies of the oil crisis of the early 1970s. Even those local authorities which saw the Act as an opportunity to make positive provision for disabled children and adults, found themselves restricted by the impact of severe budgetary constraints.

A final and major reason why the Act failed (in its own terms) concerns the issue of access, itself a major theme of this book. The Act carried with it no duty to assess the needs of individual disabled people for the services it provided. This meant that in general, only those aware of their rights and assertive enough to demand them, benefited from its provisions. For most disabled people and those close to them, however, its benefits were simply inaccessible.

Following the 1970 Act, there were no major legislative changes affecting local authority provision for disabled people for almost two decades. The 1986 Disabled Persons (Services, Consultation and Representation) Act may have appeared promising in some respects (for example, its provisions regarding advocacy for disabled people), but substantial parts of it remained unimplemented. Consequently, it has been argued that it did little other than acknowledge that disabled people should be consulted over services (Drake, 1999). It was not until the 1990 NHS and Community Care Act came fully into force in 1993 that disabled people were accorded the right to an assessment of their needs for services. Once assessed as needing a service, the disabled person had a right to the provision of that service, a right that was, however, almost immediately diluted by a 1997 House of Lords judgment in *R v Gloucestershire County Council ex parte Barry*[7]. The court ruled that a local authority could, when deciding what a disabled person needed, have regard to its own resources (ie that there was a budgetary crisis requiring cutbacks as was the case in Gloucestershire). We discuss the likely impact of the 1998 Human Rights Act on this judgment in Chapter 3.

The 1990 Act was at the heart of the community care reforms of the late 1980s and early 1990s and represented the changed agenda of the New Right, an agenda which in many respects has been further developed by New Labour (Harris, 2002). This included an enhanced role for the voluntary and private sectors in the provision of a mixed economy of healthcare, education and social care services (Holliday, 1982; McCarthy, 1989; Cochrane, 1993; Billis and Harris, 1996).

The late 1980s and early 1990s saw the Disabled People's Movement together with other lobby groups, campaigning for measures which would enable disabled people to have a greater degree of autonomy and control over their lives (Morris, 1993; Campbell and Oliver, 1996). One such measure was the option of replacing services in kind with cash payments made directly to disabled people so that they could purchase the assistance of their choice. The creation of the Independent Living Fund in 1988 paved the way for the 1996 Community

Care (Direct Payments) Act which gave local authorities the power to make payments to disabled adults in lieu of services which they had been assessed as needing. The 2000 Carers and Disabled Children Act further extended this provision to young disabled people over the age of 16 years.

Disabled children and their families

In the 30 years following the Second World War, it was not unusual for disabled children to spend their whole childhood in conditions that were depriving and unseen by the public in the long-stay hospitals (Oswin, 1998). During this period, those children living at home with their families were also a largely invisible group. They received little in the way of practical or financial support and many faced substantial hardship (see for example, Younghusband et al, 1970; Read, 2000). It was the paucity of services in the 1950s which provided the impetus for the creation (often by the families of children themselves) of a number of charities such as the Spastics Society.

While the 1944 Education Act allowed for disabled children to be educated in mainstream schools, in practice, the majority of those who were deemed educable, found themselves in separate special schooling. Some children such as those with severe learning difficulties were excluded from education altogether, until the 1970 Education (Handicapped Children) Act gave local authorities the responsibility for making provision for them.

It was only in the 1970s, as a result of the campaigns and publicity related to Thalidomide and vaccine damage, that the circumstances of disabled children and their families were accorded any real measure of attention on the public policy agenda (Baldwin and Carlisle, 1994). The general trend away from long-stay hospital care also had implications for the children who were placed there, and whose upbringing was giving rise to concern (Oswin, 1971, 1978, 1998). Tyne (1982) argues that one of the most significant achievements of the National Development Group for the Mentally Handicapped, set up by the Secretary of State at the DHSS in 1975, was to convince government that the large hospital could never be regarded as a satisfactory home for a child. It therefore, became more of a commonplace expectation for disabled children to be brought up at home by their families.

Some increased awareness of the personal and material circumstances of the children and their families, together with a growing emphasis on provision outside hospital, undoubtedly gave impetus to the introduction of a number of measures intended to support them. These included the non-contributory cash benefits discussed earlier, and in 1973, the formation of the Family Fund to give grants to families with disabled children. Despite this, a growing body of contemporary research revealed that increasing numbers of parents caring for their disabled sons and daughters at home, found that they received far from adequate community-based support (Glendinning, 1983).

The Warnock Committee (DES, 1978) heralded a major reform of education for disabled children. The 1981 Education Act introduced the concept of children with special educational needs together with the procedure that quickly became dubbed 'statementing'. Through this procedure, it was intended that an assessment and statement of a child's special educational needs would be undertaken and that this, in turn, would determine the appropriate provision – an example of the 'needs-led' approach which was to become more familiar in the field of community care in the 1990s. Unfortunately it quickly became apparent that the process was complex, protracted and costly for all concerned (Spastics Society, 1992), and failed to pave the way unequivocally for the introduction of inclusion of disabled children in mainstream schools.

In the last decade, however, as a result of amendments to the legislation and its Code of Practice (currently the 1996 Education Act Part IV and 2001 Code of Practice, and more recently as a result of the 2001 Special Needs and Disability Act Part I), inclusion has gradually become a possibility for more children, albeit one still blighted by severe underfunding and protracted administrative procedures.

The 1989 Children Act, although primarily enacted to regularise child protection procedures (including shortcomings identified by the European Convention on Human Rights in *O, H, W, R and B v UK*[8] [1987]) also had implications for disabled children and their families. The Act promoted the notion that disabled children should be included as 'children first' within legislation designed to safeguard the interests of all children. Disabled children were specifically defined as 'children in need' and a new duty was placed on local authorities to safeguard and promote their welfare and to support their upbringing by their families. The Act empowered local authorities to provide a wide range of services in order to fulfil this new duty. In the event, however, a combination of resource restrictions and the competing demands of the child protection system, meant that such family support services remained underdeveloped for all 'children in need' (DoH, 1995).

Despite significant legislative and policy change since the 1970s, research consistently questions whether these reforms have in fact resulted in disabled children and their families experiencing any sustained and positive benefit. Services remain patchy and underfunded, and many children and their families receive little in the way of support. Cash benefits still do not offset the additional costs incurred by growing up with disability. As a consequence, many, including some of those in greatest need, find themselves predominantly reliant on their own personal coping strategies and resources (Beresford, 1995; Dobson and Middleton, 1998; Gordon et al, 2000; Read and Clements, 2001).

Redefining disability issues: the impact of the Disabled People's Movement

The past 25 years have witnessed a major sea change in disability rights politics together with related social science research and other literature on disability. Not only has there been an expansion in disability-related publications but there have been significant shifts in the way that disability is theorised and understood. Increasingly disabled people themselves have won a central role in setting policy agendas and lobbying for change (Campbell and Oliver, 1996).

By the end of the 1970s and beginning of the 1980s, more publications by both disabled and non-disabled writers began to emerge, which highlighted and challenged the fragile and disadvantaged position of disabled people within the social structure (eg UPIAS, 1976; Finkelstein, 1980; Ryan and Thomas, 1980; Shearer, 1980; Walker, 1980; Sutherland, 1981; Thomas, 1982; Oliver, 1983). Within this literature, matters hitherto regarded as private and personal misfortunes, began to be redefined as public issues for which there should be a greater degree of collective responsibility.

Across the 1980s and 1990s, this process of redefining both the nature of disability and the problems encountered by disabled people was accelerated by a growing number of disabled academics within the expanding field of 'disability studies' (eg Oliver, 1983; Abberley, 1987, 1992, 1997; Barnes, 1990; Morris, 1991; Shakespeare, 1994; Campbell and Oliver, 1996). Their work both reflected and informed a strengthening Disabled People's Movement which in turn, began to have an impact on public policy and politics (Abberley, 1996; Campbell and Oliver, 1996).

Central to much of this work, was the notion that some of the most restrictive and unacceptable features of disabled people's lives were not inevitable or necessary consequences of having impairments. Rather, major problems were seen to result from social and political factors which could be changed by social and political means. It was increasingly argued that disabled people were a marginalised group who experienced discrimination and oppression because of the way that society was organised to exclude them by both crude and subtle means.

This literature and the process by which it was produced, increasingly validated the subjective experience of disabled people and enabled them to redefine themselves, their lives and aspirations in ways that frequently ran counter to dominant and orthodox assumptions, including those held by the professions responsible for providing them with services (Morris, 1991). It was argued that being disabled was different from, rather than inferior to, the experience of being non-disabled. Difference and diversity should be confirmed and upheld rather than eradicated. The case was persistently made, therefore, that the onus was not on disabled people to accommodate to social and political institutions and processes designed with non-disabled people in mind. By contrast, those social and political structures should be reformed to include disabled people and become the richer for it. Public organisations and services were among those targeted as needing to undergo radical change.

Some writers within the Disabled People's Movement pressed for more than a recognition of the impact of social contexts and the discriminatory treatment experienced by disabled people. Throughout the 1980s and 1990s, many disabled writers and activists who developed what became known as the 'social model of disability', argued for a major paradigm shift which redefined disability itself as the social restriction or oppression experienced by people living with impairment (Abberley, 1987; Morris, 1991; Oliver, 1990, 1996; Barnes, 1997). In other words, disability was seen to be socially created and extrinsic to the individual. Impairment was sometimes defined as the physical, sensory or intellectual limitations of function while disability explained the social, economic and political experiences associated with it (Morris, 1994). Some argued that it was fundamental to the social model that no causal relationship should be seen to exist between their impairments and the restrictions disabled people experience (Oliver, 1996), though such a view has been the focus of considerable debate and challenge (Crow, 1996; Lowe, 1996; Williams, 1996; Read, 1998).

Within the new politics of disability and the associated disability studies literature that developed over the last two decades of the 20th century, the conventional language which spoke of restrictive impairments and disabling medical conditions was replaced by one which spoke about oppression and discrimination, human and civil rights, and citizenship (Barton, 1996; Oliver, 1996; Morris, 1998). Disabled children and adults were no longer characterised primarily as patients, or people in need of help, but were redefined as disenfranchised citizens routinely prevented from having, or aspiring to, a quality of life enjoyed by others not living with disability (Oliver, 1996; Read and Clements, 2001). The focus was increasingly on the social and political barriers which impeded their access to the human rights taken for granted by others, and the ways that these could be dismantled individually and collectively (Bynoe et al, 1991; Campbell and Oliver, 1996). A number of the substantive issues identified as needing to be changed, are discussed in Chapter 3.

These ways of re-framing the debates around disability are of relevance to this book because they have implications for any discussion about the allocation of responsibility when explanations are being sought for the restrictions encountered by disabled individuals. Once it is questioned whether such restrictions can automatically be taken to be a justified and acceptable consequence of any impairment, the issue then becomes one of the degree, and nature of, responsibility to be placed on people and institutions external to the disabled person. Gradually, we see pressure both to introduce new law and to apply existing legislation so that greater onus is placed on the external institutions and bodies to take action to reduce the restrictions experienced. This can be seen both in the battle to introduce anti-discrimination legislation and in the application of existing human rights legislation.

Notes

[1] *In re Superintendent of Family and Child Service and Dawson* (1983) 145 DLR, (3d) 610, also reported and referred to in *In re C* [1990] Fam 26 as *In re SD* [1983] 3 WWR 618.

[2] February 1995, No 231, HMSO (1995).

[3] Lac (2000) 7.

[4] NAWC 27/2000.

[5] Para 11: Appendix H6, 'Report of a consultation conference on the capacity to consent'.

[6] Para 4.6 Law Commission Paper 'Consent in sex offences: a policy paper', February 2000 published in Appendix C to Home Office Consultation Paper 'Report of a consultation conference on the capacity to consent', 2000.

[7] 1 CCLR 40; [1997] 2 All ER 1.

[8] The texts of the various judgments all being found in volume 10 EHRR; the text of the financial settlement judgments being found in volume 13 EHRR.

TWO

The Human Rights Act and the European Convention on Human Rights: an introduction

Introduction

In this chapter we provide a brief history of European human rights law and procedures prior to the implementation of the 1998 Human Rights Act (HRA, 1998). This is intended to explain the Act's relationship with the European Convention on Human Rights and other international human rights treaties. The main body of the chapter provides an account of the substance of the Act and key procedures associated with it. This is intended to provide a basic grounding in its provisions – its scope and limitations.

In this, and succeeding chapters, reference is made to a number of legal provisions and judgments. Those readers without access to a law library, can find many of the judgments and legal provisions on the internet. We provide a note of some of the key websites as Appendix III on page 121.

The incorporation of the European Convention on Human Rights

The European Convention on Human Rights (the Convention) was finally incorporated into the domestic law of the United Kingdom on 2 October 2000. Since then its provisions and the case law of the European Court of Human Rights (the Court) can be referred to directly in British courts (Section 2 of the 1998 Human Rights Act), and so far as is possible, our courts must reach decisions that are compatible with the Convention rights (Section 3 of the 1998 Human Rights Act).

Of course, even before its incorporation, the Convention exerted a strong influence over our courts and legislature. Ever since the UK ratified the Convention in 1950 and thereby agreed to be bound by the judgments of its Court, it has shaped – proactively or reactively – our legal system. Thus a finding by the Court in 1989 that restrictions on the rights of service users to access their social services files violated Article 8 (*Gaskin v UK* [1989]) led to the injustice being remedied by the enactment of the Data Protection Act in 1998. Almost certainly, however, the Convention's greatest legislative influence has resulted from parliament's conscious effort to 'Strasbourg-proof' new legislation.

The 1998 Human Rights Act has now elevated this process to a statutory obligation; Section 19 requiring that before the second reading of a Bill the relevant Minister must make "a statement of compatibility", which is in effect formal assurance that the government addressed this question in the drafting of the Bill.

Since 2 October 2000, litigants no longer have to tread the long road to the European Court of Human Rights in Strasbourg before they can articulate their claims in the language of the Convention. They are now entitled to issue proceedings in our domestic courts (Section 7 of the 1998 Human Rights Act) if they believe that they have suffered as a consequence of a public authority acting (or indeed failing to act) in a way which is incompatible with their Convention rights (Section 6). These proceedings are generally no different from any other proceedings that are commenced in our courts and tribunals.

The Convention is primarily concerned with the relationship between individual citizens and public authorities (for example, central and local government, the police, the courts and so on): it does not seek to directly regulate the way private individuals interact with each other. While the 1998 HRA sought to widen the definition of a 'public authority' to include anybody that exercised functions of a public nature (Section 6(3)), the interpretation of the Court has, as yet, been cautious. Accordingly it has found that a large charitable provider of residential accommodation for older people is not a public authority for the purposes of the 1998 Act, and therefore not bound by its provisions[1]. Since the last 20 years have witnessed a wholesale privatisation of hitherto public functions in the health and social care sectors, it might be argued that this is a major weakness of the legislation. The courts have, however, pointed out that such organisations are vulnerable to challenge if they act against their charitable objectives, and are bound by the common law to act with humanity, both of which requirements may be little different to that imposed by the Convention. In addition public bodies have been advised to ensure that private providers of care are contractually bound to respect the Convention rights of service users.

In order to preserve the constitutional principle of parliamentary supremacy, the 1998 Human Rights Act denied judges the power to annul incompatible primary legislation. The High Court is, however, empowered to make a 'declaration of incompatibility' (Section 4 of the 1998 Human Rights Act). The Act provides that in such cases the executive may urgently amend the incompatible provision[2] (Section 10 of the 1998 Human Rights Act) although pending amendment it remains in force notwithstanding that it violates the Convention. Disgruntled litigants continue of course to have access to the Strasbourg Court in such cases.

Other human rights treaties

Although much of this text is concerned with the provisions of the European Convention on Human Rights, it must be borne in mind that this is merely one of many dozens of important international documents concerning the protection of human rights. The Convention, it is true, has a number of uniquely important attributes, that have resulted in its achieving an unequalled eminence: it is the only international Treaty in the history of humankind that guarantees the right of an individual to make a complaint that is capable of resulting in a binding judgment enforceable against a member state.

The very effectiveness of the Convention's enforcement machinery has led lawyers to place it, quite correctly, in the centre of the limelight: for lawyers recognise that rights without effective remedies are of little value. Admiration for the Convention should not however obscure its shortcomings. In general there is a trade-off between the quality of a right protected and the quality of a remedy provided. States are cautious about signing up to international treaties that have effective enforcement mechanisms, unless the rights protected are tightly defined and do not make unrealistic economic or political demands. The Convention inevitably embodies all these traits. In addition, its very age presents a problem – in the last 50 years much has changed, including social perceptions, prejudices and expectations. Problematically, therefore, it makes no reference to the rights of disabled people, of children or minorities, and when listing examples of discrimination (Article 14) omits any reference to disability. Some of these shortcomings have been remedied by the policy of the Court to treat the Convention as a 'living instrument'. By this it means that it is prepared to develop its interpretation of certain provisions to ensure they reflect current values. This has enabled the Court to develop Article 8 (the right to private and family life) to encompass the rights of children and to entrench the rights of gay and lesbian people. However, such a device can only achieve so much. No matter how enlightened and dynamic the approach of the Court may be, it depends upon actually having a concrete case before it. That, for disabled people is the key problem – the inaccessibility of the legal process.

It is against this backdrop that the relevance of 'other human rights' covenants (also variously labelled, 'treaties', 'conventions', 'declarations', 'charters' and so on) can be appreciated – of which no review, however brief, can be complete without making reference to their principle source of inspiration, namely the UN's Universal Declaration of Human Rights (UDHR). Adopted in 1948 it lists a full range of rights but provides no enforcement machinery: accordingly states have been free to sign up to it, without being obliged to do anything further. The arrangement of the rights within the UDHR and some of the rights themselves have also been the subject of criticism:

> The list is untidy and unargued. It includes some rights of high importance that perhaps are universal rights. It also includes culturally narrow rights, such as the 'right to holidays with pay': but this supposed right was an aspiration of the labour movement in the developed world in the middle of the twentieth century; and it has little relevance for the billions of human beings who are not even employees. (O'Neill, 2002)

The rights listed in the UDHR can be divided into two broad categories: those which all states have power to maintain and protect (freedom from torture, fair hearings, peaceful assembly, and so on) as opposed to those which to some extent depend upon national wealth and its distribution (that is, housing, education, food, and so on). With a view to developing the UDHR into an enforceable set of principles, these two categories have been grouped into two separate covenants (which were adopted in 1966):

- the non-economic basic rights into the International Covenant on Civil and Political Rights (ICCPR); and
- the social and economic rights into the International Covenant on Economic, Social and Cultural Rights.

Negative and positive rights

The rights listed in the ICCPR are essentially negative in nature, and for this reason amenable to judicial protection. As outlined in Chapter 1, negative rights (sometimes called 'hard' rights) are rights that in large measure depend upon the state not taking action; for instance, not killing, not torturing, not enslaving, not arbitrarily detaining and so on. Positive rights (sometimes labelled 'socio-economic' or 'soft' rights) on the other hand require action by the state. Examples would include the right to a job if unemployed, the right to a house if homeless, the right to social security if poor and so on. These are not rights protected by the ICCPR, nor indeed by the European Convention on Human Rights, since this Convention is largely a regional example of the ICCPR. Unlike the Convention, however the ICCPR has no judicial enforcement machinery. The Covenant creates a 'Human Rights Committee' to which member states must submit periodic reports concerning the measures that they are taking to implement its provisions. Additionally there is an individual right of complaint to the Human Rights Committee, however this does not result in a binding judgment of the type provided by the Strasbourg Court (and the Committee is not in any event a 'judicial body'). The individual right of complaint only exists in those states that have specifically agreed to this process (which the UK has not).

Most other international human rights documents (be they variously described as Conventions, Covenants, Resolutions or Recommendations) are generally either freestanding like the UDHR, and lacking any policing mechanism; or, like the ICCPR, rely upon member states submitting periodic reports (frequently at four-year intervals) which are then scrutinised by an international supervisory committee created by the Treaty. Although these documents attract considerable support from states (arguably because their high moral content is unaccompanied by onerous obligations) they nevertheless have a practical importance that has been explained as follows:

> Complaints to the European Commission of Human Rights are made against individual states, most of which have (in one way or another) been party to [such human rights documents].... The Court and Commission will accordingly approach the complaint on the basis that these resolutions form the benchmark of acceptable standards of state behaviour. (Clements, 1997, p 9)

It is not, of course, only the Strasbourg Court that will have regard to such human rights documents when trying to establish what justice requires in any particular instance. Our own domestic courts are increasingly prepared to consider such material: by way of example, in *R (Wilkinson) v RMO Broadmoor and MHA Commissioner and Secretary of State for Health*[3] (2001) (a case concerning the appropriateness of coercive medical treatment on a patient detained under the 1983 Mental Health Act) Lord Justice Simon Brown commented as follows:

> 28. One document usefully brought to our attention ... was a report by the European Committee for the Prevention of Torture and Inhuman and Degrading Treatment or Punishment in August 2000, paragraph 41 of which reads[4]:
>
>> 'patients should, as a matter of principle, be placed in a position to give their free and informed consent to treatment. The admission of a person to a psychiatric establishment on an involuntary basis should not be construed as authorising treatment without his consent. It follows that every competent patient, whether voluntary or involuntary, should be given the opportunity to refuse treatment or any other medical intervention. Any derogation from this fundamental principle should be based upon law and only relate to clearly and strictly defined exceptional circumstances.'
>
> 29. That gives some indication of modern thinking on this sensitive subject. ([2001] 5CCLR 121, p 133)

A list of relevant international documents concerning the rights of disabled people is provided in Appendix II.

The European Convention on Human Rights

The Convention is divided into two main parts: the first lists the substantive rights protected by the Treaty and the second deals with procedural matters, such as the creation and composition of the Court and the admissibility rules for complaints. The form and content of the Convention has been amended by various 'Protocols' since 1950. Protocols either introduce additional rights, which the Member States can adopt by ratification if they so choose, or they introduce procedural amendments to the Convention. As the number of applications grow exponentially, there have been many such procedural amendments all aimed at streamlining the complaints procedures.

The Commission and the Court

The most fundamental change to the system was wrought by Protocol 11. Prior to this there were two scrutinising bodies in Strasbourg; the Commission which vetted applications in order to assess whether they complied with the Convention's procedural admissibility criteria, including time limits, the exhaustion of domestic remedies, a 'victim' status requirement and so on (Clements et al, 1999). If these criteria were satisfied, the Commission made a decision on admissibility, and subsequently produced a report giving its advisory opinion as to whether the facts of the complaint disclosed an actual violation of the Convention. In general thereafter the case went to the second scrutinising body, the European Court of Human Rights, which then gave a final judgment in the case. As a result of Protocol 11 the Commission was abolished on 31 October 1999.

The main Convention rights

The substantive rights protected by the Convention comprise Articles 2–14 together with the three additional 'rights' under the First Protocol. These, and their relevance to disabled people, are briefly outlined below (the full text of these Articles is to be found in Appendix I. Although Article 1 does not describe a substantive right, it has become of crucial importance in the Court's interpretation of the subsequent Articles. Accordingly the following overview commences with Article 1.

Article 1 and 'positive obligations'

On the face of it, Article 1 appears to be a mere formal recital of good intent. When states ratify the Convention, by Article 1 they promise to: "secure to everyone within their jurisdiction the rights and freedoms" set out in the Convention. These rights and freedoms are, as noted above, largely negative in character: not to torture (Article 3); not to interfere in family life (Article 8); not to restrict expression (Article 10) and so on. What has transformed the Court's approach to these rights, however, has been its unique and truly imaginative determination that Article 1 creates a *positive obligation* on individual states. This can be illustrated by the Court's decision in *A v UK* (1998)[5]. The case concerned the caning of a nine-year-old boy by his stepfather with such force that it caused significant bruising. Although the stepfather was charged with causing actual bodily harm to the boy, he pleaded the defence of 'reasonable parental chastisement' and was acquitted. The case was taken to the European Court of Human Rights. The Court found that the level of injuries suffered by the boy were sufficiently severe to amount to degrading treatment contrary to

Article 3. However the negative aspect of this provision merely requires the state's representatives to refrain from inflicting such harm (for instance police officers, schoolteachers, soldiers etc). In this case the harm had been caused by a private individual, and so the question that arose, was 'How could the state be held responsible for this incident?'. The Court answered in the following terms:

> ... the obligation ... under Article 1 of the Convention to secure to everyone within their jurisdiction the rights and freedoms defined in the Convention, taken together with Article 3, requires States to take measures designed to ensure that individuals within their jurisdiction are not subjected to torture or inhuman or degrading treatment or punishment, including such ill-treatment administered by private individuals.... Children and other vulnerable individuals, in particular, are entitled to State protection, in the form of effective deterrence, against such serious breaches of personal integrity....

> ... In the Court's view, [British] law did not provide adequate protection to the applicant against treatment or punishment contrary to Article 3.... In the circumstances of the present case, the failure to provide adequate protection constitutes a violation of Article 3 of the Convention. (*A v UK* [1998], para 22)

Accordingly when the negative rights under the Convention are viewed through the prism of Article 1, they acquire a positive dimension. Rhetorically, Article 1 asks the following question: 'In such a situation, what would a state, that took its promise under Article 1 seriously, do?'. The answer to this question in the case of *A v UK* was to restrict the scope of the defence of 'reasonable parental chastisement'.

Much of this text (and in particular Chapter 4) is inevitably concerned with the extent to which courts have been prepared to impose positive obligations on the state in order to address the inherent discrimination experienced by disabled people.

Article 2: the right to life

Violations of the negative obligations under Article 2 have been found in cases such as the killing of IRA terrorists on a bombing mission to Gibraltar[6] and a failure to protect a vulnerable prisoner from a dangerous cellmate[7]. The Court has accepted that positive obligations require special measures to be taken to protect potentially suicidal patients[8] and may require individuals to be warned if exposed to any serious environmental or health risks[9]. The Commission has likewise considered the extent of the state's obligation to reduce the risks of a vaccination programme[10] or to fund a health service[11]. There are however limits to the obligation under Article 2. It cannot for instance be construed to provide a right for an incapacitated adult to have another assist her in dying (*Pretty v UK* [2002])[12].

Article 3: torture, inhuman and degrading treatment

The Court has emphasised that for treatment to be 'degrading' it must reach a minimum threshold of severity[13], although it has indicated that this may be significantly lower for disabled[14] and elderly people[15]. Arbitrary and gross acts of discrimination may exceptionally be considered to violate Article 3, even in the absence of actual physical or mental harm[16]. The negative obligations under Article 3 are engaged by police brutality[17], the birching of criminals[18], corporal punishment of children in schools[19] and poor prison conditions[20]. Extradition may violate Article 3 if the expelled person is thereby put at risk of degrading treatment (even if solely a consequence of inadequate medical treatment in the receiving country)[21].

As noted above (*A v UK*) Article 3 has been construed as creating a positive obligation on states to ensure that no one suffers from degrading treatment. Accordingly courts and social services are obliged to use their powers to protect children[22] and vulnerable adults[23] from abuse. Where credible evidence exists that an individual has suffered abuse whilst in the care of a public authority, a positive obligation arises under Article 3 for an independent and open investigation to be convened[24].

Article 4: slavery and forced labour

No violation has yet been found of Article 4(1) (slavery) and very few under 4(2)[25] (forced or compulsory labour). For Article 4 to be violated the work must be compulsory, thus unpaid work per se does not come within this provision.

Article 5: deprivation of liberty

Article 5(1) places a total prohibition upon a state's power to detain people except in six clearly defined instances. Article 5(1)(e) is of particular relevance in this context because it applies to 'persons of unsound mind', which the Court has interpreted as encompassing people with learning disabilities as well as mental health service users. A substantial body of case law exists concerning the Convention requirements that must be satisfied before a mental health service user can be legally detained, and the 1983 Mental Health Act was largely a response to a number of adverse Strasbourg judgments[26]. Increasingly the Court is requiring detention under this ground to be accompanied by a suitably therapeutic environment[27].

Article 6: the right to a fair hearing

Almost half of all the Strasbourg judgments concern Article 6, which provides for the right to a fair hearing in civil or criminal proceedings. In such cases Article 6(1) requires that there be access to a 'fair' hearing, in 'public' 'within a reasonable period of time' before an 'independent and impartial tribunal or court'. These are substantial rights, but unfortunately the European Court of Human Rights has failed to provide a coherent explanation as to what it means by a 'civil right' (Herberg et al, 2001).

Civil rights

It is difficult to explain succinctly what the Strasbourg Court means by 'civil rights', particularly since the ascribed meaning is materially different from the way the word is used in the UK – where it is generally used to mean a legal dispute that is not 'criminal'. The Strasbourg meaning is narrower, largely excluding what are sometimes referred to as administrative or public law rights. The rights of 'private persons' in their relations between themselves in, for instance, employment, property and commercial law are always 'civil'. A 'civil' dispute must generally be something that could be the subject of proceedings in the County Court, or before the relevant social security or planning or employment tribunal. Other disputes directly involving arguments about money may also be considered 'civil' disputes, however, many administrative or public 'rights', are not considered 'civil' rights. Thus a dispute concerning a child's education is not considered a civil dispute[28] (although it engages a Convention right – Article 2 of the First Protocol), whereas a dispute about social security benefits is considered civil[29].

Article 7: retrospective criminal laws

Article 7 prohibits the creation of new criminal offences which have retrospective application, and likewise, prohibits the retrospective application of increased sentencing powers.

Article 8: respect for private and family life, home and correspondence

Even before the Court adopted its dynamic application of Article 1 to develop the concept of positive obligations underlying Convention rights, it had consistently defined Article 8 as positive in nature[30]. This arises out of the presence of the word 'respect': rather than obliging states 'not to interfere' with private and family life etc, Article 8(1) enjoins states to 'respect' these conditions. The demonstration of 'respect' is inherently positive in nature. While family life, the home and correspondence have been given their everyday meanings, the concept of 'private life' has acquired an altogether more expansive interpretation, including a 'person's physical and psychological integrity' for which respect is due in order to "ensure the development, without outside interference, of the personality of each individual in his relations with other human beings"[31]. Thus issues of sexual rights[32], environmental pollution[33], physical barriers to movement[34], access to files[35] and information about one's illness[36] have been held to come within its reach.

Article 9: freedom of thought, conscience and religion

Although the Court has "deliberately adopted a broad approach" (Starmer, 1999) to its interpretation of the beliefs protected by Article 9, it has nevertheless been invoked in relatively few complaints; of these most have involved religion, prison restriction and conscientious objection.

Article 10: freedom of expression

The Court has, so far, shown little enthusiasm for reading into Article 10, substantial positive obligations, notwithstanding that it protects, not merely freedom of expression, but also the right to "hold opinions and to receive and impart information". At present the Court views the obligation on the state as largely negative, namely not to "restrict a person from receiving information that others wish or may be willing to impart to him"[37]. One of the most important Article 10 judgments remains *Sunday Times v UK* (1979)[38]; which concerned the attempt to suppress newspaper coverage of the Thalidomide compensation litigation.

Article 11: freedom of assembly and association

Cases raising Article 11 have been dominated by disputes concerning public assemblies, marches and trade unions (to which Article 11 specifically refers). The freedom to 'associate' however is potentially of great importance to disabled people; although as yet there has been no clarification as to what precisely this aspect of the concept of 'association' encompasses. The Court has however ruled that in relation to prisoners, it does not include the right to share the company of others[39].

Article 12: the right to marry

Article 12 may be seen as one aspect of the Article 8 right to family life[40]. Whereas Article 8(2) details a number of restrictions upon the exercise of the substantive Article 8 right, the right to marry is subject only to the person being of marriageable age, and that the exercise of the right be "subject to the national laws governing the exercise of this right".

Article 13: the right to a remedy

Article 13 entitles anyone who believes their Convention rights have been violated to obtain an appropriate and effective domestic remedy. The provision is designed to ensure that violations of the Convention are remedied by individual states rather than in Strasbourg. Article 13 clearly overlaps with Article 6 (the right to a fair hearing). However, it applies in all cases when Convention rights are involved, whereas the full procedural rights under Article 6 are only obligatory in criminal and civil cases. Thus a dispute about a child's schooling engages a Convention right (Article 2 of the First Protocol), but not (as noted above) a 'civil' right. Article 13 requires that in such cases there be an effective remedy, although this may not be a totally independent hearing in public and so on (as required by Article 6). Of course in the UK, there is provision for such an independent tribunal for disputes about Special Educational Needs (SEN), namely via the SEN Tribunal. However disputes concerning a child's exclusion from school (for example, for bad behaviour) are not heard before a fully independent panel under the provisions of the 1998 School Standards and Framework Act.

Any failure to provide an effective remedy (contrary to Article 13) is only capable of challenge by complaint to Strasbourg, since Article 13 was not incorporated into UK law via the 1998 Human Rights Act (Section 1(1))[41].

Article 14: freedom from discrimination

Article 14, like Article 13, can only be invoked in relation to one of the substantive rights set out in Articles 2–12 of the Convention and the Protocols. Article 14 requires that in the delivery of the substantive rights, there be no discrimination. Unlike Article 13, it does not require an arguable violation of a substantive right before it applies; merely the existence of a real and unjustified discrimination between the way certain individuals are permitted to enjoy that right. Discrimination is permissible under Article 14, if it is established that the measure has an objective and reasonable justification and is 'proportionate' (as discussed below).

Protocol I, Article I: the enjoyment of one's possessions

Article 1 of Protocol 1 affirms that every "natural or legal person is entitled to the peaceful enjoyment of his possessions". 'Possessions' have been broadly defined by the court to include not only money, land, personal assets and social security benefits[42], but also any interest with an economic value. In relation to the right, it has been noted that it is:

> ... frequently invoked but violations are seldom found; given that the permissible restrictions are so widely drawn, this is not surprising. In such cases, the Court often finds a violation of an ancillary Article, most frequently Article 6(1); the Court then finds the interference justified but not the way in which it was carried out. (Clements et al, 1999, p 223)

Protocol I, Article 2: the right to education

Article 2 is phrased as a negative right, namely "no person shall be denied the right to education". It does not therefore oblige the state to provide this education, but where (as in the UK) it does, then it requires that it "respect the right of parents to ensure such education and teaching in conformity with their own religious and philosophical convictions". Again this does not place an absolute obligation on the state, since it is required to 'respect' parental views, rather than being bound to comply with them. The Court has considered a number of complaints from parents seeking to have their children educated within mainstream education as well as from parents seeking particular forms of education, and these are reviewed in Chapter 3.

Protocol I, Article 3: the right to elections

Article 3 of the First Protocol provides a weak obligation on the state to ensure that there are frequent and fair elections "by secret ballot, under conditions which will ensure the free expression of the opinion of the people in the choice of the legislature". The Court has permitted restrictions on eligibility to vote, but stressed that they must not "... curtail the rights in question to such an extent as to impair their very essence and deprive them of their effectiveness, that they are imposed in pursuit of a legitimate aim; and that the means employed are not disproportionate"[43].

Absolute and qualified rights

The substantive Articles of the Convention can be divided into two broad categories: those whose rights are 'absolute' and those that are 'qualified'. Absolute rights cannot be restricted or qualified in any way. Article 3, for instance, states that "no-one shall be subjected to torture or to inhuman or degrading treatment or punishment". It contains no proviso; and accordingly the only defence available to a state alleged to have violated it, is denial. Classically, Articles 2-7 are considered to be 'absolute'. Indeed the rights under Articles 2, 4(1) and 7 cannot be infringed even in times of war or civil emergency (permitted in relation to the remainder by Article 15, and known as 'derogation').

The majority of the rights in the Convention are however 'qualified' in the sense that the state is allowed to interfere with them in certain situations. Thus the right under Article 8 to respect for private and family life, home and correspondence, can be interfered with, for instance if the family is abusing a child, or the home is being used for illegal purposes and so on. Likewise the right to freedom of expression can be restricted if a person is giving away state secrets or inciting people to race hatred and so on. Any interference with a 'qualified' right must be sanctioned by domestic law, must pursue one of the 'legitimate aims' stated in the Article itself (for example, national security, public safety and so on) and must be no more than strictly necessary. This latter requirement has become known as the principle of 'proportionality'.

Proportionality

The principle of 'proportionality' is fundamental to the Convention. It is concerned with the striking of a fair balance between conflicting legitimate interests – usually conflicts between the general interest of the community as a whole, as opposed to the interests of separate individuals.

It has been suggested that proportionality is best understood by considering a number of criteria or questions (Fordham and de la Mare, 2001) which include:

- *Effectiveness*
  Is the measure a 'suitable' means of achieving the legitimate aim? Does it actually achieve its stated aim?

- *Is it the least intrusive interference possible?*
  Can the objective of the measure be achieved by means which are less restrictive of individual rights?

- *Does the interference deprive the person of the 'very essence of the right'?*
  Does the interference effectively deprive the individual of the whole of the right, or merely curtail one aspect of its enjoyment?

- *Balance*
  Effectively this requires the measure to be looked at 'in the round', and an assessment made as to whether it really does strike a fair balance between the demands of the general community and the interests of the person concerned[44].

The jurisprudence of the European Court of Human Rights has, therefore, evolved through an imaginative and purposive interpretation of the individual Articles so as to ensure that the Convention remains a living instrument of relevance to the needs of Europeans today. In relation to the application of the Convention's positive obligations and qualified rights, the increasingly sophisticated legal instrument of 'proportionality' has become the legal principle of overriding importance.

Notes

[1] *R v Leonard Cheshire Foundation and HM Attorney General ex parte Heather and Callin* (2002) CA [2001] 4 All ER 604; [2001] 3 WLR 183.

[2] As indeed occurred as a result of the declaration of incompatibility in *R v MHRT, North and East London Region and the Secretary of State for Health, ex parte H* (2001) *The Times*, 2 April; [2001] HRLR 752; [2001] 3 WLR 512; a case concerning Section 72 of the 1983 Mental Health Act which placed the burden of proof being on the

detained patient to establish grounds for discharge rather than obliging the hospital to prove that detention was necessary.

[3] [2001] EWCA Civ 1545; 5 CCLR 121 at 133.

[4] These comments can be found in a resume report prepared by the European Committee for the Prevention of Torture which summarises key themes that emerge from its various country reports. This report is entitled 'Substantive Sections of the CPT's General reports' and can be accessed via the internet at www.cpt.coe.int/en/. The precise quote is at page 31 of this report.

[5] 100/1997/884/1096; 23 September 1998.

[6] *McCann v UK* (1995) 21 EHRR 97.

[7] *Edwards v UK* (2002) *The Times*, 1 April.

[8] *Keenan v UK* (2001) *The Times*, 18 April; 33 EHRR 39.

[9] *LCB v UK* (1998); 27 EHRR 212.

[10] *Association X v UK* (1978) DR 14/31.

[11] *Osman v UK* (1998) *The Times*, 5 November; [1999] Crim LR 82; 29.

[12] EHRR 245; (1998) 29 EHRR 245.12 35 EHRR 1; and see also domestic proceedings at [2001] 3 WLR 1598: [2002] 1 All ER 1.

[13] *Costello-Roberts v UK* (1993) 19 EHRR 105.

[14] *Price v UK* (2001) *The Times*, 13 August: 34 EHRR 1285.

[15] See *Papon v France* 7 June 2001 an inadmissibility decision.

[16] *Patel v UK (the East Africans case)* (1973) 3 EHRR 76.

[17] *Ribbitsch v Austria* (1995) 21 EHRR 573.

[18] *Tyrer v UK* (1978) 2 EHHR 16.

[19] *Campbell and Cosans v UK* (1982) 2 EHRR 293.

[20] *Napier v Scottish Minister* (2001) *The Times*, 15 November and see also *Price v UK* (2001) *The Times*, 13 August: 34 EHRR 1285.

[21] *D v UK* (1997) 24 EHRR 423.

[22] *Z and others v UK* (2001), *The Times*, 31 May; (2002) 34 EHRR 97.

[23] *In re F (adult: court's jurisdiction)* (2000) 3 CCLR 210; *The Times*, 25 July.

[24] *Assenov v Bulgaria* (1998) 28 EHRR 652; see also *Labita v Italy* 6/4/2000.

[25] *Schmidt v Germany* (1994) 18 EHRR 513.

[26] See for instance, *X v UK* (1981) 4 EHRR 188; and *Ashingdane v UK* (1985) 7 EHRR 528 and *Winterwerp v the Netherlands* (1979) 2 EHRR 387.

[27] *Michel Aerts v Belgium* (1998) 29 EHRR 50.

[28] *R v Alperton Community School and others ex parte B and others* (2001) *The Times*, 8 June.

[29] *Schuler-Zgraggen v Switzerland* (1995) 16 EHRR 405.

[30] *Marckx v Belgium* (1979) 2 EHRR 330.

[31] *Botta v Italy* (1998) 153/1996/772/973; 24 February 1998.

[32] *Norris v Ireland* 13 EHRR 186 (1988).

[33] *Hatton v UK* (2001) 34 EHRR 1.

[34] *Botta v Italy* (1998) 153/1996/772/973; 24 February 1998.

[35] *Gaskin v UK* 12 EHRR 36 (1989).

[36] *McGinley and Egan v UK* (1998) 27 EHRR 1; and *LCB v UK* (1998) 27 EHRR 212.

[37] *Leander v Sweden* (1987) 9 EHRR 433; and *Guerra v Italy* (1998) 26 EHRR 357.

[38] 2 EHRR 245.

[39] *Bollan v UK* (2000) 42117/98; 4 May 2000; see also *McFeeley v UK* (1980) 8317/78; 15 May 1980; 20 DR 44.

[40] But does not oblige the state to provide prisoners with access to artificial inseminations; *R v Secretary of State Home Department ex parte Mellor* (2000) *The Times*, 5 September.

[41] See for instance *In re S and W (children: care plan)* (2002) *The Times*, 15 March: [2002] 2 WLR 720; [2002] 2 All ER 192.

[42] *Gaygusuz v Austria* (1996) 23 EHRR 364.

[43] *Mathieu-Mohin and Clerfaut v Belgium* (1987) 10 EHRR 1; 2 March 1987.

[44] *Soering v UK* (1989) 11 EHRR 439.

THREE

Disabled people's human rights: developing social awareness

Introduction

This chapter describes the ways in which the language of human rights has, over the last two decades, come to the fore in disability politics, policy and research in the UK. It reviews a number of factors that have been identified as impacting on disabled people's human rights together with key concepts which have emerged over this period to explain the social mechanisms that underlie these factors.

Some of these issues have been addressed in Chapter 1, not least the process of redefinition by which the question of discrimination has been brought into the foreground. As we have suggested, through the related discourses, disabled children and adults are defined less as patients in need of help or cure, and more as disenfranchised citizens experiencing discrimination and oppression. Consequently, many experiences which were hitherto regarded as inevitable, and negative consequences of impairment are redrawn as unacceptable and unnecessary discrimination – as violations of human rights.

Access and barriers to access

The increased focus on the limiting nature of the context external to the disabled person has brought into frequent use the overarching, twin concepts of access and barriers to access. The notion of reducing barriers and creating social and physical environments and processes that are accessible to, and usable by, disabled people, has been increasingly recognised and developed since the 1970s (Zarb, 1995). It has also been acknowledged that restricted access in one area can create a barrier to access and participation in another. The telling photograph on the cover of *The politics of disablement* (Oliver, 1990), shows a wheelchair user at the bottom of a flight of steps leading to the entrance to a polling station. It is also acknowledged that experiences frequently associated with disability such as poverty, may also compound and magnify many of the barriers to access which disabled people face. Not being able to afford driving lessons and a suitable car, may leave an individual reliant on a public transport system which still has enormous barriers to access and use by disabled people.

The use of these concepts is widespread and is applied to a range of diverse circumstances. Perhaps the use that is familiar to most people is in relation to the built environment and transport. It can also be applied in relation to a much broader range of concepts and experiences affecting an individual's quality of life. For example, writing in an earlier work on disabled children's quality of life and human rights, the authors suggested:

> Our approach is founded on a very simple assumption. We believe that it should not be regarded as an exotic idea for disabled children and those close to them to aspire to a quality of life comparable to that enjoyed by others who do not live with disability.... We should therefore never start from the assumption that an experience which is taken for granted by many non-disabled children and their families should be ruled out on the grounds of a child being disabled. By contrast, if we start out by assuming that disabled children and their families should have access to experiences which others routinely expect, the issue then becomes one of finding the route to achieve it and the services that will enable it to happen. (Read and Clements, 2001, pp 14-15)

In short, we are suggesting widening the use of access to include processes, facilities, experiences and choices which might go some way to placing disabled children and adults on a par with their non-disabled peers.

Any consideration of the application of human rights law to the issues that impact on disabled people's lives must inevitably address the problems of accessing the justice system, let alone accessing 'justice'. Any redress to be had through the application of the law is, in part, dependent on disabled people having access to the process, an issue which we shall discuss in some detail in Chapters 4 and 5. There is considerable evidence that different groups within the population have differential access to the law, and that poor people, although over represented as defendants in the civil and criminal justice processes (and as victims in the latter) are effectively excluded from many of the benefits of the 'rule of law' (Wexler, 1970; Genugten and Perez-Bustillo, 2001; Robson and Kjønstad, 2001). It has to be remembered that as a group, disabled people are seriously disadvantaged financially and are frequently living in poverty or on its margins (Bertoud et al, 1993; Dobson and Middleton, 1998; Gordon et al, 2000).

Poverty and material hardship

While it is important to consider the way that socio-economic status is associated with differential access to due process, the poverty and material hardship experienced by very many disabled people is also an issue which merits attention in its own right. It has long been established that the presence of a disabled child or adult has a significant financial impact on a household (Baldwin, 1985; Bertoud et al, 1993; Dobson and Middleton, 1998). This comes about as a result of two main factors. Costs of living with disability are high and therefore so is expenditure. At the same time, however, the opportunities for adults to earn income outside the home are reduced. Not only do disabled adults themselves have more restricted labour market participation (Barnes et al, 1998) but those giving care and assistance to a disabled child or adult also have restricted employment opportunities (Beresford, 1995; Lawton, 1998; Holzhausen and Perlman, 2000). As a consequence, there is an increased risk of those living with disability finding themselves in poverty or on its margins. A substantial number of disabled children and their families are quite simply "the poorest of the poor" (Gordon et al, 2000, p 246).

The right to life and access to healthcare

A series of crucial issues which centre in different ways on the value accorded to disabled children and adults have been the subject of debate in the UK over the past two decades at least. They have been concerned with the right to life of disabled children and adults, their right to medical treatment to preserve life, with abortion on the grounds of impairment, and with the prevention and cure of impairment.

There is one issue above all which illuminates the fragile position of disabled people within the social structure. As we have seen, over the past two decades, there have been recurring debates, which have at their core the question as to whether some have the right to life on the same basis as non-disabled people. As we indicated in Chapter 1, these public debates have often been linked to legal disputes in the UK and the US, such as the case of Baby Alexandra in 1980, and the trial of Dr Leonard Arthur in 1981. Shearer (1984) makes a compelling argument that these cases together with the public, legal and professional debates associated with them, indicate forcefully the lower value which many accord to disabled people.

Such matters were also considered by a more recent independent inquiry into the outcomes of paediatric cardiac services at two London hospitals (Evans, 2001). The terms of reference of the Evans Report included an investigation into alleged discrimination and inappropriate attitudes towards children with Down's syndrome by those responsible for delivering cardiac services. While the panel found no evidence of discrimination in the treatment that was delivered, it concluded that in some cases, children were less favoured in accessing treatment by reason of their Down's syndrome. It summarised conflicting perceptions of discriminatory attitudes as follows:

> The majority of families we saw felt that communication in their child's case was at some time either inappropriate or insensitive. Remarks alleged to have been made by the staff carried for the parents the implication that children with Down's syndrome were of less value to society, or were less suitable recipients of scant NHS resources than other children. The doctors are insistent that such insensitive remarks or inappropriate attitudes would not have occurred. (Evans, 2001a, p 42, para 130)

A number of writers have also drawn attention to the implications for disabled people of the ideology which underpins the fact that the likelihood of a child being disabled, in itself constitutes grounds for termination of pregnancy (Oliver, 1990). Again, it is suggested that this underscores the widely-held belief that to be disabled is to be of less value than being able-bodied. For related reasons, some have also argued against genetic engineering, and medical and other interventions, aimed at eradicating, preventing or curing impairment, believing this to be at best undermining to disabled people and at worst, genocidal (for example, Abberley, 1997).

Of course, by no means do all disabled people feel able to celebrate disability as 'difference', nor regard cure, amelioration or prevention of impairment as being undesirable (Booth, 1992; Read, 1998). It is not difficult, however, to understand why this set of issues should be regarded by many as so significant. Any preventative or curative interventions seen to be based on uncritical and dominant notions of normality, may undermine efforts to validate the authenticity of a different way of being and in the end, may be seen to carry with them negative personal, social and political consequences for those who fall outside the definition of what it is to be normal. In some circumstances, as we have seen, it proves only to be a very short journey from being defined as abnormal to the point of being stripped of the fundamental rights enjoyed by those who remain within the dominant category.

Abuse, restriction and degrading treatment

While the general public and the social and healthcare professions have long been aware of the need to protect children in general from abuse and neglect (Stevenson, 1989; DoH, 1995), it was not until the 1990s that disabled children had anything other than a shadowy presence on the child protection agenda. From this time, research began to highlight a number of key concerns about their safety and well-being (Cross, 1992; Kennedy, 1992, 1996; Marchant and Page, 1992; Westcott, 1993, 1998).

From such work, a number of themes emerge about disabled children's particular vulnerability to abuse in institutional settings or elsewhere. For example, they often have to rely on a number of people for intimate care and assistance. Both the numbers of carers involved, and the nature of this contact may serve to mask abusive or exploitative practices. Some disabled children may have difficulty in making themselves understood and it may, therefore, prove hard for them to let others know of abusive experiences without some form of mediation. Their relative isolation from other children and adults, and their reduced opportunities for unassisted social contact, may make it easier for abuse and neglect to remain hidden. Some disabled children may also grow up to accept damaging, demeaning or over-restricting treatment from others simply because they have never known or been offered something more positive and humane.

It has been argued that this general vulnerability may be magnified for children living in some residential settings away from their families. This may be a particular danger if they are out of touch with those who know them well or if they have no trustworthy key person taking responsibility for their present and future well-being (Read and Clements, 2001; Read and Harrison, 2002). In addition, there has been considerable debate about the fact that in some institutional settings, standards of care, routine practices and quality of life more generally are so poor that they may be regarded as abusive and an infringement of disabled children's human rights (Morris, 1998c).

It is not only children who may be victims of abuse. In Chapter 1, we discussed the revelations of ill-treatment and depriving conditions endured by some adults with learning disabilities detained in long-stay hospitals in the 1960s (DHSS, 1969). It is only in the last decade, however, that awareness has grown substantially about the abuse that may be inflicted on disabled and other vulnerable adults in their own homes or in residential settings (Brown and Craft, 1989; Morris, 1993; Alzheimer's Society, 1998). In addition, research has highlighted the restriction and powerlessness that many disabled adults routinely experience when receiving residential or home care (Morris, 1993). It was forcefully argued by many from within the Disabled People's Movement that the price to be paid for essential assistance was unwarranted restriction and a loss of choice and autonomy. What was called 'care' was frequently experienced as control by another name (Morris, 1993; Fitzgerald, 1998; Smith, 1998).

As we have seen, the imperative to act on the growing recognition of the nature and extent of abuse of vulnerable adults culminated in the publication of Department of Health policy guidance on the development of multi-agency protection policies and procedures (DoH and the Home Office, 2000). It is indicative of an increased awareness of the concept of human rights, that the guidance defines abuse as "a violation of an individual's human and civil rights by any other person or persons" (DoH and the Home Office, 2000, p 9). Within this definition, a wide spectrum of forms of abuse are identified. They include physical, sexual, psychological and financial or material abuse. Acts of omission, neglect and discrimination are encompassed. Attention is drawn to the way in which poor care or unsatisfactory professional practice may sometimes be at a level that it should be defined as institutional abuse.

Even when not defined as abusive, the restriction and lack of choice and control that was seen frequently to go hand-in-hand with being a user of domiciliary and residential provision *in kind*, has been a cause of great concern to many disabled people (Morris, 1993). It was one of the factors that gave the impetus for moves to enable disabled people to receive direct payments from local authorities so that they could purchase and manage their own assistance in ways that suited them (Hassler et al, 1999). Such initiatives are not merely to do with the reduction of negative and restricting barriers, important as that may be. They are also part of a broader movement to establish that disabled people should be afforded the right and the means to exercise positive choices and to access a comparable quality of life to that of their non-disabled peers.

Family, home and private life

Personal, private and family life is clearly one such area of crucial importance to disabled people and there is substantial evidence that in these respects, the experiences of disabled children and adults diverge considerably from those of their non-disabled peers.

While the majority (91.2%) of disabled children live at home with their parents for most of their childhood, a significant minority spend substantial periods away from their families (OPCS, 1989). It is clear that this population of children undoubtedly have a far greater chance than non-disabled children of spending some proportion of their childhood living away from home (Gordon et al, 2000; Read and Harrison, 2002). In the early 1990s, important findings became available on the patterns of care of disabled children living in communal establishments (Loughran et al, 1992). The re-analysis by Loughran et al of the 1980s OPCS data highlighted important trends in the care of disabled children living away from home, as well as significant limitations of the information available about their circumstances. For example, the chance of a disabled child (as defined by the OPCS studies), spending time in local authority care was ten times greater than that which prevailed among the child population as a whole (Gordon et al, 2000). By the mid-1990s, it was becoming apparent that a comprehensive reassessment was needed of the experiences, quality of life and standards of care for disabled children separated from their families of origin (Morris, 1995, 1998a, 1998b; Russell, 1995; Ball, 1998).

Disabled children can be found in a range of settings such as hospitals and other health service establishments, local authority or independent sector residential establishments, substitute family placement, and residential schools. Some appear to use residential and family-based short-term break provision, not as one part of a community-based child and family support service but rather as an element of a substantial, mixed package of provision, primarily based away from home. A disturbing number lose contact with their family and friends (Gordon et al, 2000), and may find themselves rather adrift in the system (Morris, 1995). Retrospective accounts by disabled adults offer insights into what it means to become dislocated from family and community (Humphries and Gordon, 1992; Smith, 1994; French, 1996). In recent years, there has been increasing research and debate about the experience of these children, but it is widely recognised that information is still less than satisfactory (Ball, 1998; Knight, 1998; Morris, 1998a; Abbott et al, 2000; Gordon et al, 2000; Read and Clements, 2001; Read and Harrison, 2002).

While it may be the case that in some circumstances and at some points in the lifecourse, good quality residential care, or boarding school for example, may be a positive choice for both child and family, it can hardly be assumed that this is so for all of the disproportionately large numbers who are placed away from home. It is imperative to consider the circumstances which make living away from home a positive choice rather than one which is brought about, say, by a lack of decent community care support (Russell, 1995). If the choice is indeed positive, it is still essential to consider the arrangements which need to be in place so that it does not result in an unwarranted schism between the child and family.

As disabled children reach adulthood, there is evidence that they face a range of barriers which conspire to inhibit the creation of, or participation in, an independent personal, private, and family life comparable to that to which other adults of a similar age can aspire (Hirst and Baldwin, 1994). Just as it is important to acknowledge that non-disabled young people and adults have a range of lifestyles which they accept or aspire to, it is equally important to recognise that independence, home, and family life will vary in its meaning and take different forms for disabled people (Read and Clements, 2001). If given real choice, some might wish to live separately from their families of origin while others might not. Some might aspire to a place of their own while for others, group living would seem a positive option. Some would wish to become parents while others would not, and so on. What is clear from research, however, is that many are significantly disadvantaged in terms of quality of life choices and outcomes compared with other young people and adults (Morris, 1993; Hirst and Baldwin, 1994; Fitzgerald, 1998).

While the nature of their impairments may be one significant factor, research suggests that the restricted experiences which many have, are not a necessary consequence of them (Hirst and Baldwin, 1994). The introduction of appropriate supports and opportunities can be a mediating factor that enhances the quality of life outcome immeasurably. Hirst and Baldwin (1994) argue that the degree of autonomy to which a disabled young adult may aspire, has to be understood with reference to a complex interrelationship between impairment, social disadvantage and available opportunities. Other writers too, document the ways in which social forces and institutional structures present disabled young people and adults with social, economic and physical barriers which deny them equal opportunities and the ordinary markers of citizenship. Current limitations on community care services, suitable housing and accommodation, may trap them and their families into styles of living that they would not otherwise choose, whether those be at home or in residential care (Morris, 1993, 1999a, b; Barnardo's Policy Development Unit, 1996; Oldman and Beresford, 1998; Simons, 1998; Harker and King, 1999).

Increasingly, attention has been drawn to the ways in which a range of environmental, economic and attitudinal factors also restrict the opportunities for disabled young people and adults to explore their sexuality and to develop sexual relationships (Barnes, 1990; Hirst and Baldwin, 1994; Lonsdale, 1994; Shakespeare et al, 1996). Lonsdale describes how disabled women are as likely as anyone else to internalise society's dominant values about what is regarded as sexually attractive, and this may have negative consequences for those regarded as outside the norm. In addition, she argues that they are widely regarded by others as not coming within the category of those who establish 'sexual eligibility' (Lonsdale, 1990, p 7). While some are assumed to be a-sexual, others have been subjected to pressure to undergo sterilisation precisely because they are perceived as sexually active (Barnes, 1990). The latter applies particularly to women with learning disabilities. As Lonsdale (1990) points out, they can simultaneously experience the extremes of social isolation and invasion of privacy.

It has also been argued that disabled people have frequently faced significant prejudice, misunderstanding, over-intervention or lack of support both in relation to their wish to become parents in the first place and in relation to the way that they are seen to discharge their parental responsibilities (Finger, 1991; Mason, 1992; Booth and Booth, 1994; Keith and Morris, 1996; Wates, 2001). While childcare and health professionals undoubtedly need to ensure that children's needs are paramount, there are serious concerns raised by research about whether disabled adults with children have been offered the appropriate opportunities and supports which would enable them to become, and remain, 'good-enough' parents.

Social life, association, segregation and communication

In the main, disabled children and adults perhaps face greater barriers in developing social relationships and friendships than those who are able-bodied (Barnes, 1990; Sloper et al, 1990; Hirst and Baldwin, 1994; Beresford et al, 1996; Cavet, 1998). Formative and sustaining social contact is no less important for disabled children and adults but a number of factors are prone to inhibit it.

Children often form friendships based on contact made at school. If, as is sometimes the case, disabled children are at a special school outside their neighbourhood, it may be difficult without assistance, to maintain those friendships out of school hours. Families often play a crucial mediating role in the children's social lives by arranging social contacts, and play and leisure activities for those who have difficulty doing it for themselves spontaneously (Beresford et al, 1996). This, however, requires money, transport, time and energy, commodities on which there are already considerable demands, in many hard-pressed families with disabled children (Beresford, 1995; Dobson and Middleton, 1998).

Many disabled adults may face similar difficulties in making spontaneous social relationships without the assistance of others (Barnes, 1990). Those who remain with their families of origin beyond childhood and who do not have support services in their own right, may also remain reliant upon their parents for assistance in this respect. They may also find that their social relations are inextricably bound up with those of their informal carers. Many adults use the workplace as a main location for meeting and making friends. Unfortunately, the number of interrelated factors which restrict employment opportunities for disabled adults (Barnes et al, 1998; Kestenbaum, 1998; Simons, 1998; Read and Clements, 2001), mean that this opportunity is precluded for many.

A further issue which affects all aspects and levels of the social interactions of disabled children and adults is the degree to which they are able to communicate with others. This is a question which has been neglected in the lives of many but which has been given increased attention during recent times (Beecher,

1998; Morris, 1998c, 2002; Russell, 1998). Where there are difficulties in communication, the children concerned have a far greater chance than their non-disabled peers of having someone make decisions on their behalf. They are less likely to be consulted about the things that radically affect them and to be able to express preference or dissent. Their social life is likely to be more restricted and confining. In considering the position of these children, a rather simple question needs to be borne in mind: 'If we were to come to the conclusion that it would be unbearable and damaging for a non-disabled child to be without a satisfactory means of communication or a consistent way of expressing preference or dissent, how can it be regarded as acceptable for a disabled child?' (Read and Clements, 2001).

The issues of segregation and social exclusion have been of enormous concern to disabled people and those close to them. Clearly many of the experiences that we have already highlighted have exclusionary dimensions. Central to the concern about segregation of any sort, is the notion that the segregated person is not usually in the position of choosing something different, equal or better. They are seen to have no choice but to be separated from the mainstream in a way that has a negative impact on the quality of their lives directly or indirectly.

As we have seen, the placement of disabled children and adults in long-stay hospitals, sometimes for a lifetime, was common practice until relatively recent times (Booth et al, 1990; Ward, 1990; Oswin, 1998). The damaging effects of this type of segregated institutional living have been well-documented (Oswin, 1971, 1978; Ryan and Thomas, 1980).

Since the late 1970s and early 1980s, there has also been a growing challenge to the established wisdom that it was necessary and desirable for disabled children to be educated separately from their non-disabled peers (Barton, 1986; Barnes, 1990; Booth et al, 1992; Reisser and Mason, 1992; DfEE, 1998; Booth, 1999). It has been argued that the segregated education system has reproduced and maintained the disadvantaged position of disabled people in a variety of ways. It has also been suggested that the system has played a major part in ensuring that disabled children were set on a course of segregation and disadvantage that would continue for the rest of their lives, and that the quality of education on offer was frequently inferior in quality and of narrower dimensions. This state of affairs saw to it that many would be unprepared for employment and an independent adult life. It has been argued that mainstream education must change to include a more diverse range of pupils (Booth, 1999). As would be expected, disabled people and their families do not hold uniform opinions on the appropriateness of mainstream or separate education (Dobson and Middleton, 1998; Shaw, 1998).

Research and other literature have increasingly identified features of disabled people's everyday lives as fundamental breaches of human rights. The aim of the next section of the book is to test out the extent to which the European Convention on Human Rights and the Human Rights Act can address such matters.

FOUR

Human rights cases – disabled people: a detailed analysis (UK, European and international)

Introduction

This chapter seeks to identify and review those court and tribunal decisions that are of direct relevance to the human rights of disabled people. Primarily these are judgments of the European Court of Human Rights, although reference is also made to the increasing body of case law emerging from our own domestic courts on this issue. Where relevant, reference is also made to decisions of constitutional courts in other jurisdictions, which although not binding on British courts are increasingly being considered as persuasive when a new or difficult question of law arises. Before embarking on this analysis it is important to address what is perhaps a central theme of this text: namely the reasons why there have been comparatively few complaints by disabled people to the Strasbourg Court.

The issue of access

Rights without remedies are hypothetical and illusory. For the rights embodied in instruments such as the European Convention on Human Rights, to be a concrete reality in the lives of disabled people, they must be accompanied by accessible and effective enforcement mechanisms.

In practice, however, many legal remedies are anything but accessible to disabled people. The obstacles to access take many of the traditional forms highlighted by the proponents of the social model of disability. They include physical barriers to older court buildings, the imposition of particular rules for people considered to lack mental capacity, the lack of adequate advocacy and legal aid support as well as the attitudes of lawyers and administrators. A measure of the problem is the dearth of complaints by disabled people to the Court in Strasbourg[1] – explicable only in terms of the severe impediments disabled people face in gaining access to the civil justice process. It may indeed be that the severity of impairment bears a direct relationship with the severity of the impediment encountered[2].

One of the earliest Strasbourg judgments concerning access to the civil justice process concerned restrictions placed upon the access of prisoners to lawyers, *Golder v UK* (1975)[3]. In this case, the UK argued that although the relevant Article of the Convention, Article 6(1), guaranteed the right to a fair hearing it did not oblige the state to enable applicants to have access to lawyers/ advocates in order to instigate the civil process. So long as the right to a fair hearing existed, it was of no consequence that it was founded at the apex of an inaccessible ivory tower.

The Court rejected this approach commenting "one can scarcely conceive of the rule of law without there being a possibility of having access to the courts", and that: "Just as the Convention presupposes the existence of courts, as well as legislative and administrative bodies, so does it also presuppose, in principle, the existence of the right of access to the courts in civil matters; for without such a right no civil court could begin to operate".

Access to effective remedies is, of course, precisely what is denied to many disabled people. On occasions the restriction is patent: for example the inability of a person made subject to appointeeship[4] to challenge the decision before an independent tribunal. However, in general the denial of access to effective remedies is less blatant. The procedures involved are simply not sensitive to the needs of people who may be exhausted, in pain or overwhelmed, who frequently have an ingrained feeling of powerlessness, who may be very short of information and who may also fear the repercussions of making a complaint (Simons, 1995).

The obligation to ensure an equality of access to the right to a 'fair hearing' inevitably requires states to take positive measures in relation to disadvantaged groups. The facts of *Skjoldager v Sweden* (1995)[5] convey an early and disappointing failure by the Commission to grasp the extent of the problem. The applicant, a psychologist, as part of his employment visited a care home for disabled people where he found a number of them to be unlawfully locked in their rooms. As a result of his report, action was taken that eventually resulted in the locks being removed. Where unlawful detention (contrary to Article 5(1)) has occurred, Article 5(5) requires that compensation be paid. None was forthcoming and the applicant complained to the European Commission in Strasbourg. He did so in a representative capacity and in his own name, since the municipality had refused to disclose the residents' names to him: it not being disputed that the residents were incapable of lodging the complaint themselves.

Regrettably the Commission dealt with the application in a purely mechanistic way, on the basis that the applicant had neither specific authority to make the complaint on behalf of the disabled patients, nor had he "shown that the patients were unable to lodge an application in their own names". Since the applicant had been denied access to the patients it is difficult to see how he could have garnered such evidence. The Commission, by this decision, suggests that provided disabled people are kept incommunicado, violations of their Convention rights can be suppressed. A more imaginative approach, however, was taken by the Commission in *SP, DP and T v UK* (1996)[6] which concerned young children. Their parents had abandoned them and so there appeared to be no one authorised to bring their complaint to Strasbourg. A lawyer who had previously been involved in their case made the complaint even though the children were no longer his clients. The Commission overruled the UK government's objections to this lack of authority, stating "a restrictive or technical approach in this area is to be avoided" because children "must generally rely on other persons to present their claims and represent their interests and may not be of an age or capacity to authorise steps to be taken on their behalf in any real sense".

As is evident from the *Skjoldager* complaint, many disabled people must also (to a greater or lesser degree) rely upon third parties to 'represent their claims'. This relationship, however, even when recognised by domestic courts, can itself create procedural barriers for the disabled person.

In *Egger v Austria* (1993)[7] the Commission considered an application by a complainant with learning disabilities, who was in dispute with the guardian appointed to represent him by the domestic Austrian courts. He alleged that the restriction on his ability to litigate, and the refusal to change his guardian, amounted to an unjustified interference with his rights under Article 6(1) (to have a fair hearing in relation to his civil rights). The Commission considered that although "the right of access to court is not absolute but may be subject to limitations", nevertheless "the limitations applied must not restrict or reduce the access left to the individual in such a way or to such an extent as to impair the very essence of the right".

On analysis, the Commission found that effective supervision of guardianship did exist in Austria and accordingly no violation of Article 6(1) had occurred. However in the analogous case of *Matter v Slovakia* (1999)[8] the Court held that excessive delay in the process for appointing (and challenging) guardians did violate the applicant's rights under Article 6(1) (fair hearing).

The Commission also found the process unreasonable in *JT v UK* (1997)[9]. On the applicant's detention under the 1983 Mental Health Act, her mother was automatically appointed as her 'nearest relative', and as such, had significant powers, including access to confidential information and an ability to make strategic decisions concerning her continued detention. The applicant strongly objected to the appointment. She and her mother had a difficult relationship and she had made repeated assertions of sexual abuse by her stepfather. The Commission concluded that these facts amounted to a violation of the applicant's right to privacy (Article 8).

For many disabled people, their access to justice is not so much frustrated by the imposition of an unwanted representative, but rather by the absence of any support or assistance. The preponderance of disabled people living in poverty is itself a material factor in this equation: if there is no obligation on the state to provide assistance for people too poor to pay for it themselves, then this will impact disproportionately on disabled people.

To what extent therefore does the Convention require the state to make available such assistance? In *Airey v Ireland* (1979)[10] the applicant wished to be legally separated from her violent husband. In Ireland this required her to initiate complex proceedings in the High Court. She considered proceedings of this nature to be beyond her ability, she could not afford a lawyer, and legal aid was not available for such proceedings.

In the Court's view she could only have 'access to a fair hearing' if the state provided her with legal assistance (or simplified the judicial separation process). The Irish Government challenged this interpretation on the ground that Mrs Airey's problem was not due to an "act on the part of the authorities but solely from [her] personal circumstances, a matter for which Ireland cannot be held responsible under the Convention". This was a somewhat disingenuous argument given that the state (that is, the National Parliament and/or the Irish judiciary) had created the complex process in the first place. However in many respects it encapsulates the traditional functional view of disability: that (paraphrasing the case) it was Mrs Airey's disability that impaired her access to the justice system, rather than any defect in the system itself. The Court rejected this argument, holding that:

> ... the fulfilment of a duty under the Convention on occasion necessitates some positive action on the part of the State; in such circumstances, the State cannot simply remain passive.... The obligation to secure an effective right of access to the courts falls into this category of duty. (para 25)

The provision of a legal aid scheme is only one of several possible responses to the problems experienced by people with an impaired ability to self-advocate. Alternatives include the possibility of simplifying the civil justice process and the provision of non-lawyer advocates. Indeed the need for a wider availability of advocacy services appears to be an inevitable response to the 1998 Human Rights Act. It is doubtful, however, whether the positive obligations under the Convention presently require a statutory scheme (of the type envisaged by the Disabled Persons [1986] Services, Consultation and Representation Act[11]). In *Egger v Austria* (1993)[12], for instance, the Commission held that:

> Article 6(1) ... cannot be interpreted as including an unlimited right to have an ad hoc guardian or other ad hoc representative appointed for the purpose of pursuing the intended court action.

Accordingly, at this stage the present significant, albeit piecemeal, proposals for the development of advocacy services in England, may be deemed adequate[13].

For a hearing to be fair, Article 6(1) requires (among other things) that the arbiter be independent and impartial. In *R (Beeson) v Dorset County Council* (2001)[14], the High Court held that a local authority complaints panel was not 'independent' for the purposes of Article 6(1) as it included an officer and councillor of the authority about which the complaint had been made. Likewise a judge who had stated that the European Convention on Human Rights was for 'crackpots', and that suspected drug dealers should not have rights of privacy, was not an 'impartial' arbiter in a case involving suspected drug dealers who sought to raise arguments under the Convention[15]. What, however, if the judicial partiality is merely reflective of a more general prejudice against disabled people by society?

In *Malone v UK* (1996)[16] the Commission considered a complaint by a person who, as a result of her rheumatoid arthritis, was a wheelchair user. Ms Malone alleged that possession proceedings relating to her council house were unfair. Her request that the proceedings be transferred to a nearby court had been refused, so that she had to leave home at 4.30 am to get to court on time entailing a 950-kilometre round trip. The journey had caused her severe discomfort such that she was confined to bed for four days thereafter and required medical assistance. She also complained that the court building lacked adequate lifts (she had to be carried up the steps of the court), and that she experienced excruciating discomfort due to the lack of suitable toilet facilities.

In an unsatisfactory decision the Commission declared the complaint inadmissible. It placed great weight on the fact that she had only asked for the case to be transferred to a more convenient court at a late stage of the proceedings and that she had "failed to appropriately bring to the attention of the court her difficulties"[17].

While it is incumbent upon all parties to litigation to use best endeavours to explain the problems they are experiencing (or likely to experience) this does not absolve the state of its duty to take positive measures to ensure that discrimination of this nature does not occur. The local authority taking the eviction proceedings must have known that she was a disabled person and courts must also have responsibilities (with over eight million disabled people living in the UK) to take proactive measures. Equal treatment is not a special dispensation available only if booked in advance.

In England and Wales the Judicial Studies Board has, to its credit, taken steps to draw these concerns to the attention of judges (see Chapter 5 where this guidance is further considered). The High Court has reinforced the importance of this guidance in the *R v Isleworth Crown Court ex parte King* [2001][18]. The case concerned the conviction of a disabled man, who three years earlier had had a serious stroke which had left him with brain damage. It "had a marked effect on his ability to work, concentrate and remember things". On the day of his hearing he felt pressurised by the judge to go ahead even though he had already had to wait over six hours in court.

Lord Justice Brooke quashed the conviction, noting that:

> Article 6 of the European Convention on Human Rights and the jurisprudence of the Strasbourg Court underline the importance of fairness in court procedure. ... The general scene of a person under disability, seeking to appeal against a criminal conviction, being kept waiting between 10 am and 4 pm and then having a hearing in which the court expressed itself willing to go on sitting into the evening, was a scenario which a court would be wise to avoid once the disability of the Appellant had been drawn to its attention. (para 44)

The judge also drew specific attention to the Judicial Studies Guidance stating "this advice is important advice which every judge and every justice of the peace is under a duty to take into account when hearing a case involving people with one disability or another".

In addition to such 'generic' barriers to disabled people in the civil justice process, there are many specific and technical obstacles – detailed analysis of which is beyond the scope of this text. According to Clements (2000), however:

- "the absence of clear legal principles relating to the making of decisions on behalf of people who lack sufficient mental capacity due to the failure of successive governments to implement the Law Commission's proposals on 'Mental Incapacity'" (Law Commission, 1995; Lord Chancellor's Department, 1997, 1999);
- practical difficulties are created by the Civil Procedure Rules that oblige people with limited mental capacity to act through a third party (known as a 'litigation friend');
- the requirement that 'litigation friends' give the court a personal undertaking to be responsible for the costs of the proceedings[19];
- unreasonable restrictions on advocates accessing the files of their partners/clients who have been deemed incapable of managing their own affairs.

Healthcare and the right to life

Although the provisions of Article 2, protecting 'everyone's' right to life, have been of direct relevance to disabled people, ever since the UK ratified the Convention over 50 years ago, it is only in the very recent past that its potential implications have begun to be appreciated.

As the Commission asserted as long ago as 1978 in *Association X v UK*[20] (a case where it was alleged that a vaccination programme endangered the lives of children), the 'right to life' provision in the Convention (Article 2) requires "states not only to refrain from taking life intentionally but, further, to take appropriate steps to safeguard life".

For the purposes of this book, it is the extent of the twin limits to this positive obligation that is of greatest interest. What is the scope of the obligation to provide healthcare, and at what point does its provision become oppressive?

The positive obligation to provide healthcare

While the negative prohibition under Article 2 is absolute and unqualified, this is not the case in relation to its positive obligations[21]. In *Osman v UK* (1998)[22] (a case where it was alleged that the police had taken insufficient measures to protect a father and son known to be at serious risk) the Commission, in its preliminary opinion, speculated as to the extent of this obligation, in the following terms[23]:

> ... the extent of this obligation will vary inevitably having regard to the
> source and degree of danger and the means available to combat it. Whether
> risk to life derives from disease, environmental factors or from the intentional
> activities of those acting outside the law, there will be a range of policy
> decisions, relating, inter alia, to the use of State resources, which it will be
> for Contracting States to assess on the basis of their aims and priorities,
> subject to these being compatible with the values of democratic societies
> and the fundamental rights guaranteed in the Convention ... the extent of
> the obligation to take preventive steps may however increase in relation to
> the immediacy of the risk to life. Where there is a real and imminent risk to
> life to an identified person or group of persons, a failure by State authorities
> to take appropriate steps may disclose a violation of the right to protection
> of life by law.

The effect of this approach is to place on the state the burden of justifying its
failure to act where that failure presents a 'real and imminent risk to life'. A case
of particular relevance in this situation arose prior to the coming into force of
the 1998 Human Rights Act. *R v Cambridge Health Authority ex parte B* (1995)[24]
concerned a decision not to fund further chemotherapy treatment for a young
girl. The health authority took the view that the treatment had a low chance of
success, would be disproportionately expensive and cause considerable distress
to the patient. In the High Court Mr Justice Laws criticised the authority's
justification for its decision as consisting "only of grave and well-rounded
generalities", stating that:

> ... where the question is whether the life of a 10-year-old child might be
> saved, however slim a chance, the responsible authority ... must do more than
> toll the bell of tight resources ... they must explain the priorities that have led
> them to decline to fund the treatment.

The Court of Appeal felt unable to sustain this line, holding instead:

> Difficult and agonising judgments have to be made as to how a limited budget
> is best allocated to the maximum advantage of the maximum number of
> patients. That is not a judgment which the court can make.... It is not
> something that a health authority ... can be fairly criticised for not advancing
> before the court....

With the enactment of the 1998 Human Rights Act it may be that the Court
of Appeal's judgment is no longer tenable, and the views of Mr Justice Laws are
to be preferred. Neither he nor the Commission in the *Osman* case were
saying that in every case a state must expend disproportionate resources protecting
the lives of its vulnerable members. What it must do, however, is have rational
policies that ensure that its resources are applied in an equitable and even-
handed way, consistent with "the values of democratic societies and the

fundamental rights guaranteed in the Convention". Arguably this is the raison d'etre of the National Institute for Clinical Excellence[25]: to ensure that policies on access to treatments and drugs are based on rational analysis and not subject to the vagaries of postcode lotteries[26] and local assessments of efficacy.

The courts have accepted that their scrutiny of such decisions has, post 1998 HRA, become more rigorous or 'heightened'[27].

The legal implications of the extreme treatment decisions considered in the Dr Leonard Arthur trial (see Chapter 1) have been addressed by our domestic courts without direct recourse to the Convention[28]. In *Re J (a minor) (wardship: medical treatment)* (1990)[29] the Court of Appeal reviewed the law, in the context of a decision concerning the future treatment of a six-month-old child. Medically he was described as very severely brain damaged, likely to be paraplegic and unable to sit up or to hold his head upright; he was blind and deaf, and it was highly unlikely that he would develop even limited intellectual abilities. However it was considered likely that his ability to feel pain was not impaired. The child had stopped breathing and been artificially ventilated on a number of occasions, and the question for the court was whether the doctors could withhold further treatment, should this recur. The parents and doctors were largely in agreement, that in such a situation further treatment would not be in the child's best interest. Lord Donaldson took as the starting point of his analysis a quote from the judgment of McKenzie J of the Supreme Court of British Columbia[30]:

> I do not think that it lies within the prerogative of any parent or of this court to look down upon a disadvantaged person and judge the quality of that person's life to be so low as not to be deserving of continuance ... [and that it was] ... not appropriate for an external decision maker to apply his standards of what constitutes a liveable life and exercise the right to impose death if that standard is not met in his estimation. The decision can only be made in the context of the disabled person viewing the worthwhileness or otherwise of his life in its own context as a disabled person....

Applying the relevant principles, Lord Donaldson concluded that the only perspective, could be that of the patient, as this:

> ... gives effect, as it should, to the fact that even very severely handicapped people find a quality of life rewarding which to the unhandicapped may seem manifestly intolerable. People have an amazing adaptability. But in the end there will be cases in which the answer must be that it is not in the interests of the child to subject it to treatment which will cause increased suffering and produce no commensurate benefit, giving the fullest possible weight to the child's, and mankind's, desire to survive[31].

One of the questions addressed by the House of Lords in the subsequent case of *Airedale NHS Trust v Bland* (1993)[32] concerned the cost implications of maintaining the treatment (in the case of Anthony Bland he had been in a persistent vegetative state since the Hillsborough football ground tragedy in April 1989). Lord Browne-Wilkinson, however, emphasised that in such extreme situations:

> ... it is not legitimate ... to take into account the wider practical issues as to allocation of limited financial resources or the impact on third parties of altering the time at which death occurs.

Although the *Bland* decision pre-dated the 1998 Human Rights Act, the courts have since concluded that the relevant principles there applied, satisfy the positive obligations created by Article 2 of the Convention[33]. This must be the case; for instance in *Edwards v UK* (2002) the European Court of Human Rights stated that "the scope of the positive obligation [under Article 2] must be interpreted in a way which does not impose an impossible or disproportionate burden on the authorities".

The duty to provide medication

The Court and Commission have recently considered complaints, concerning restrictions on the state subsidy of essential medication. If, as appears likely, the Commission's view in the *Osman* decision (discussed above) reflects the Court's current approach, then the extent of the obligation to provide healthcare services "will increase in relation to the immediacy of the risk to life". In this respect, therefore, the Court's decision in *Netecki v Poland* (2002)[34] would appear harsh. The Polish system only provided for a 70% contribution towards the cost of the drug used to treat the applicant's amyotrophic lateral sclerosis. He alleged that he could not afford to pay the balance, that as a consequence his condition had deteriorated and that it was inevitable that this would result in his untimely death. The Court accepted that the positive obligation under Article 2 could be engaged in such cases, but after reviewing the facts, ruled the application inadmissible, on the basis that:

> Bearing in mind the medical treatment and facilities provided to the applicant, including a refund of the greater part of the cost of the required drug, the Court considers that the respondent State cannot be said, in the special circumstances of the present case, to have failed to discharge its obligations under Article 2 by not paying the remaining 30% of the drug price.

A similar outcome, on different facts, occurred in *Scialacqua v Italy* (1998)[35]. The applicant was diagnosed as requiring a liver transplant. Instead he sought help from a herbalist whose treatment proved successful. The applicant's request for a refund from the Italian health service was refused since the herbal medicines were not listed in the official 'medicines list'. In holding the complaint inadmissible, the Commission stated:

> Even assuming that Article 2 ... can be interpreted as imposing on states the obligation to cover the costs of certain medical treatments of medicines that are essential in order to save lives, the Commission considers that this provision cannot be interpreted as requiring states to provide financial covering for medicines which are not listed as officially recognised medicines.

Potentially oppressive healthcare treatments

The principles articulated in the *Re J* and *Bland* decisions, discussed above, have been applied and developed by domestic courts when assessing the legality of 'positive' treatment decisions. Thus in a 1997 case the Court was asked to sanction treatment which would allow a bone marrow transplant from an adult whose learning disabilities were such that she was quite incapable of giving her consent: the transplant had been deemed medically essential to save her sister's life. The Court held that:

> The test to be applied in a case such as this is to ask whether the evidence shows that it is in the best interests of the defendant for such procedures to take place. The fact that such a process would obviously benefit the plaintiff is not relevant unless, as a result of the defendant helping the plaintiff in that way, the best interests of the defendant are served.

Likewise when asked to adjudicate upon the legality of sterilisation operations involving adults lacking the necessary mental capacity to consent, the Court has repeatedly asserted that the test was the 'best interests' of the patient alone and in such cases the least invasive option was always to be preferred[36].

Domestic law is equally clear that, with the exception of detained patients, adults who have sufficient mental capacity to make informed decisions cannot be treated against their wishes, even if the consequence of the decision is death (as it was in *Ms B v An NHS Hospital Trust* [2002][37] which concerned the patient's objection to being given artificial ventilation).

Less clear is the extent of the obligation on the state to ensure that patients are fully informed of the side effects of medication. In *Grare v France* (1992)[38] for instance, the applicant alleged that the side effects of medication he received constituted degrading treatment. These included involuntary shaking/trembling, blurred vision and hypertension. On the facts the Commission concluded that "nothing indicated that the treatment had attained a level of gravity to fall within the scope of Article 3". This is a somewhat surprising finding, and in view of more recent decisions concerning the state's obligations to warn of health dangers[39], and of what (for a disabled person) constitutes degrading treatment (see *Price v UK*, discussed below) it may be that a similar fact case might receive closer consideration by the Court today.

Different considerations apply where the unwelcome treatment is provided to a child or detained psychiatric patient. *Re M (child: refusal of medical treatment)* (1999)[40] concerned an intelligent 15-year-old girl whose doctors concluded that the only way to save her life was a heart transplant, but she refused to give her consent. The Court held that in such cases, and notwithstanding the gravity of the situation in overriding her wishes it was able to do so on the basis of a 'best interests' decision.

Patients detained under the provisions of the 1983 Mental Health Act who have sufficient mental capacity to make informed treatment decisions have the right to refuse any treatment which cannot be deemed to be connected with their mental disorder. Force-feeding can however be considered 'treatment for a mental disorder'[41] but normally surgery cannot[42]. In *Herczegfalvy v Austria* (1992)[43] the Court rejected a complaint by a detained patient that the treatment he had been subjected to violated Article 3 (degrading treatment), on the grounds, among others, that it conformed "to the psychiatric principles generally accepted at the time". However, this approach has been modified by a recent domestic Court of Appeal decision where it was argued (on the particular facts) that the forcible administration of medication could not be categorised as 'treatment for a mental disorder' and in any event was life threatening. In such a situation the Court held that the treatment could not be given without the patient having the opportunity to challenge the decision at a hearing at which the relevant specialists were available to be cross-examined[44].

A core set of irreducible positive healthcare obligations

In this section we have focused on two fundamental socio-legal healthcare questions: the extent of the human right to be, or not to be, treated. Although central questions, they are only two elements of the evolving and multifaceted human rights debate. Access to healthcare services has been articulated in the language of human rights in other contexts and other continents. The Department of Health has, for instance, issued guidance (HSC 2000/028) drawing attention to the potential for conflict between hospitals' 'do not resuscitate policies', in relation to older people and their positive obligations under Article 2. In *D v UK* (1997)[45] the proposed deportation of a convicted cocaine smuggler to his native island of St Kitts was held to violate Article 3. While in prison in the UK, he had been diagnosed and subsequently treated for HIV/AIDS. The Court accepted that once deported he would receive no medical treatment and inevitably die in distressing circumstances that would amount to inhuman treatment.

Other facets of the debate have been exposed by cases that have, for instance, challenged the removal of a patient from her 'home' within a long-stay hospital[46] (articulated as an Article 8 right to 'respect' for one's home) and challenged an unreasonably long waiting list for hospital treatment (articulated as an Article 8 right to 'respect' for ones physical and psychological integrity)[47]. In the US, the Supreme Court has identified similar principles as underpinning the Constitution. In *Estelle v Gamble* (1976)[48], for example, it held that deliberate indifference to serious medical needs would violate the "evolving standards of decency" protected by the Eighth Amendment (that forbids cruel and unusual punishments). In similar terms in South Africa, a right to emergency healthcare treatment has been held to be enforceable[49].

The question arises, therefore, as to whether the essentially civil and political rights under the Convention have evolved to such an extent that they now enshrine a core set of irreducible, essentially socio-economic rights – foremost of which being the right to essential healthcare services.

Since the categorisation of rights as either socio-economic or civil and political is an entirely artificial construct, it is inevitable that their boundaries are unclear – if not shifting. As the European Court of Human Rights noted as long ago as 1979 in *Airey v Ireland*[50]:

> ... the further realisation of social and economic rights is largely dependent on the situation – notably financial – reigning in the State in question. On the other hand, the Convention must be interpreted in the light of present-day conditions ... and it is designed to safeguard the individual in a real and practical way as regards those areas with which it deals.... While the Convention sets forth what are essentially civil and political rights, many of them have implications of a social or economic nature. The Court therefore considers ... that the mere fact that an interpretation of the Convention may extend into the sphere of social and economic rights should not be a decisive factor against such an interpretation; there is no water-tight division separating that sphere from the field covered by the Convention.

The question is topical (see for instance Witting, 2001) since it concerns the extent to which judges should decide how national resources should be prioritised and applied, an issue that is considered further below. However, of particular interest in this context are comments made by Lord Hoffman in the 2001 Commercial Bar (COMBAR) lecture (Hoffman, 2001): a Law Lord with well-publicised reservations about the Strasbourg process (Hoffman, 1999). In his opinion there is a core set of 'positive' justiciable, resource-dependent rights[51], which would include "a positive obligation upon the State to provide every citizen with certain basic necessities which he requires in order to be able to function as a human being" (para 24).

What then are the parameters? It appears that the greater the immediacy of the risk to life[52], the greater this core right to healthcare is, and would almost certainly extend beyond the mere right to emergency healthcare services[53]. Where healthcare is being provided, then its withdrawal cannot be sanctioned solely on financial grounds, if death[54] or degrading treatment[55] will result. Any healthcare decision (or omission) that is likely to have a serious impact on the patient's health must, at the very least, be justified on proportionate[56] grounds and in the context of clearly formulated rational[57] priorities[58]. In certain cases (as yet undefined, but including disputed psychiatric interventions) the patient should have the opportunity to test the impugned decision by cross-examining the relevant specialists[59].

Social care and freedom from abuse

As with the issue of healthcare, the extent to which there can be said to be a Convention right to social care services is determined by the scope of the positive obligations that apply to the key Convention rights (primarily Articles 2 and 3). In simple terms these can be considered by asking the question: 'What will be the consequences, if social care is not provided?'. The state's positive obligation may be engaged, if the answer is – 'a serious risk of harm' (be it through neglect, destitution or deliberate abuse). In addition, and arising inescapably from this line of reasoning, the Court has developed the notion of a 'procedural obligation', which is considered separately below.

Social action to prevent destitution and neglect

Prior to the 1998 Human Rights Act a positive obligation to provide basic care services had been developed ad hoc, primarily in response to the particular problems experienced by certain ostracised groups. The basic principle has been credited to a decision of Lord Ellenborough CJ in *R v Inhabitants of Eastbourne* (1803)[60] where he invoked the "law of humanity, which is anterior to all positive laws" and held that this required the state to provide relief for destitute foreigners.

More recently the principle has become known as the 'humanitarian safety net'[61] and it has been described as a measure of 'last resort' to ensure the provision of at least a modicum of shelter[62], warmth and food[63]. The relationship between this obligation and that under Article 3 (degrading treatment) was considered by Collins J[64] in *R (Othman) v SS Work and Pensions* (2001) where he expressed the view that the social care entitlements, under the principle of common humanity, are greater than what he regarded as the utterly minimalist rights under Article 3 (essentially to stave off starvation and serious illness). While the approach to Article 3 in *Price v UK*, discussed below, may call this assessment into question, it is largely academic, so long as the 'humanitarian safety net' principle is applied.

Perhaps the clearest expression as to when this positive obligation comes into play, was provided by McCowan LJ in *R v Gloucestershire County Council ex parte Mahfood* (1995)[65] when he gave as an example of the positive (non-resource-dependent) obligation to provide social services – situations where "persons would be at severe physical risk if they were unable to have [such services]". However, since the extent of this obligation is inextricably linked with the 'resource question' it is further analysed below under that heading.

The state's responsibility to prevent physical abuse

Z and others v UK (2001)[66] concerned four children who had been severely abused while living with their parents. The European Court of Human Rights found that there had been a violation of Article 3, because the relevant local authority "had been aware of the serious ill-treatment ... over a period of years ... and failed to take any effective steps to bring it to an end". In so deciding, the Court stated that the obligation under the Convention (Articles 1 and 3) required states:

> ... to take measures designed to ensure that individuals ... are not subjected to ... degrading treatment ... [which measures should] ... provide effective protection, in particular, of children and other vulnerable persons and include reasonable steps to prevent ill-treatment of which the authorities had or ought to have had knowledge.

The implications of this judgment for disabled adults are of course of great importance, given the widespread physical and sexual abuse they experience (Home Office, 2000, para 0.17). A major problem faced by social services departments, and other public servants when confronted with evidence of adult abuse, has of course been the absence of legislation to facilitate effective action. As we have noted in Chapter 1, successive governments have failed to implement a statutory protection regime of the kind proposed by the Law Commission in its 1995 Report 'Mental Incapacity'[67], and some have argued that as yet there is little evidence to suggest that the government's limited initiative in this field (the Policy Guidance *No secrets* [DoH and the Home Office, 2000] and *In safe hands* in Wales [National Assembly for Wales, 2000]) has been in any way effective (Matthew et al, 2002). As has also been noted, in *A v UK* (1998)[68] (which concerned the caning of a nine-year-old boy by his stepfather), the Strasbourg Court has held states responsible for deficiencies in their domestic law when fundamental rights are at stake.

The response of the Court of Appeal to this lacuna has, of late, been imaginative, and again drawn heavily upon the potential flexibility of the common law. The key case[69] concerned a young adult who lacked sufficient mental capacity to make informed decisions as to where she should live or who posed a risk to her safety. As a minor she had been abused while in the care of her parents and accordingly been made a ward of the court and placed in specialist accommodation. The wardship came to an end on her 18th birthday and the authority feared that without some form of fresh court order her mother would seek her return home where she would be at risk of further abuse. As Dame Butler-Sloss observed, "There is an obvious gap in the framework of care for mentally incapacitated adults. If the court cannot act ... this vulnerable young woman would be left at serious risk....".

To fill this gap, the Court's solution was for it to 'grow' and 'shape' the common law principle of 'necessity'; or as Sedley LJ expressed it, "to speak where Parliament ... was silent" (p 226). In essence, the Court decided that it had the power to make 'declarations' as to where the young woman should live and who she should be protected from seeing: in reality, a new adult wardship jurisdiction, to which application can now be made when sufficient evidence of a risk of ill-treatment has been accumulated.

In *X and Y v Netherlands* (1985)[70] the Court held that the positive obligation on states in cases of abuse will also, in general, require the prosecution of the perpetrator. The case involved a complaint by a father and his adult disabled daughter concerning her rape while living at a privately run care home. Although the assailant was identified, the police were unable to prosecute because of defects in the Dutch legal system: the problem being that victims aged over 16 had to make the formal police complaint themselves. Since Y lacked the necessary intellectual capacity to do this, no criminal proceedings were possible. Accordingly Y's abuse went unpunished. In finding a violation, the Court held that in such cases there was a positive obligation under Article 8 to prosecute, and that:

> ... the protection afforded by the civil law in the case of wrongdoing of the kind inflicted on Miss Y is insufficient. This is a case where fundamental values and essential aspects of private life are at stake. Effective deterrence is indispensable in this area and it can be achieved only by criminal-law provisions....

The state as abuser

Degrading treatment can on occasions, wittingly or unwittingly, be inflicted by the state. *Price v UK* (2001)[71] concerned a Thalidomide-impaired applicant who, in the course of debt recovery proceedings, refused to answer questions put to her and was committed to prison for seven days for contempt of court. She alleged that she suffered degrading treatment as a result of the prison's inadequate facilities, but the UK government argued that any discomfort she experienced had not reached the minimum level of severity required by Article 3. The Court, however, considered that the threshold depended "on all the circumstances of the case, such as the duration of the treatment, its physical and mental effects and, in some cases, the sex, age and state of health of the victim", and after a thorough review it concluded:

> ... that to detain a severely disabled person in conditions where she is dangerously cold, risks developing sores because her bed is too hard or unreachable, and is unable to go to the toilet or keep clean without the greatest of difficulty, constitutes degrading treatment contrary to Article 3.

Of particular interest was the concurring Opinion of Judge Greve, in which he stated:

It is obvious that restraining any non-disabled person to the applicant's level of ability to move and assist herself, for even a limited period of time, would amount to inhuman and degrading treatment – possibly torture. In a civilised country like the United Kingdom, society considers it not only appropriate but a basic humane concern to try to ameliorate and compensate for the disabilities faced by a person in the applicant's situation. In my opinion, these compensatory measures come to form part of the disabled person's bodily integrity.

It has been argued that the closure of long-stay units for the care of older people can, as an indirect consequence, engage the state's obligations under Articles 2, 3 and 8. Evidence suggests that relocating institutionalised elderly people to a new residence may have a dramatic effect on their mental health and life expectancy[72], with some research studies suggesting that the increase in mortality rates might be as high as 35%[73]. Recognising this danger guidance on the 'transfer of frail elderly patients to other long-stay settings' (HSC 1998/048) was issued by the Department of Health, and includes (at para 21) acceptance that such transfers may be "stressful, however good the new surroundings". It continues:

> For a frail older patient such a move can be a serious threat to their physical, psychological and social wellbeing. It is very important, therefore, to be aware of the risks, to handle the process sensitively and to be prepared to delay or halt a transfer if necessary.

R v North and East Devon Health Authority ex parte Coughlan (1999)[74] concerned the closure of a long-stay unit and one of the applicant's arguments concerned the impact of a forced removal upon her health. Having already ruled in her favour on other grounds, the Court found it unnecessary to determine this particular issue, but nevertheless commented:

> Miss Coughlan views the possible loss of her accommodation ... as life-threatening. While this may be putting the reality too high, we can readily see why it seems so to her; and we accept, on what is effectively uncontested evidence, that an enforced move of this kind will be emotionally devastating and seriously anti-therapeutic.

A procedural 'investigative' obligation

The Strasbourg Court has additionally held that the positive obligation inherent in Articles 2 and 3 obliges states to conduct independent investigations where credible evidence exists that a person in their care has been subjected to abuse. Although the cases principally concern police/security force brutality[75], the obligation applies with equal force to allegations that (for instance) a person has been abused while in a care home. A failure to conduct a properly independent and rigorous investigation will itself constitute a violation of Article 3.

The reasoning for such an obligation is straightforward, and arises from the frequently impossible evidential burden borne by victims, or whistle blowers, in proving their claims; given that the alleged perpetrators will often (by virtue of their official position) have access to, and control of, the key evidence. The obligation will be so much the greater when the victim is, for instance, a person with learning disabilities.

Where there is credible evidence that a disabled person has been abused while in a care home or other such setting, the question that requires asking (as noted in Chapter 2) is: 'In such a situation, what would a state, that took its promise under Article 1 seriously, do?'. The answer must be, that it would hold an independent inquiry, with the alleged victim of the abuse (and to the extent appropriate to his/her advocates and family and so on), having proper access to the evidence, papers, and witnesses and so on, so as to test the thoroughness of the investigation. As the Court noted in *Assenov v Bulgaria* (1998)[76]:

> This investigation ... should be capable of leading to the identification and
> punishment of those responsible.... If this were not the case, the general legal
> prohibition of torture and inhuman and degrading treatment and punishment,
> despite its fundamental importance ... would be ineffective in practice and it
> would be possible in some cases for agents of the State to abuse the rights of
> those within their control with virtual impunity.

Detention

Although Article 5 is entitled 'liberty and security', the case law has confined its scope to the question of detention. In the context of the rights of disabled people, Article 5(1)(e) has become the provision of greatest relevance, for reasons discussed in Chapter 2. Article 5(1)(e) permits the lawful detention of (among others) 'persons of unsound mind' provided such detention is authorised and regulated by a 'procedure prescribed' by domestic law.

As noted at the outset of this text, Strasbourg applications by patients detained in psychiatric wards constitute the one significant exception to the general dearth of complaints by disabled people; this exception in many ways proving the rule: such patients do not have the 'access' problems experienced by many disabled people, since the Convention itself requires that they have a right to legal representation. In *Megyeri v Germany* (1992)[77] the Court explained that the "importance of what is at stake ... – personal liberty – taken together with the very nature of his affliction – diminished mental capacity – compel this conclusion". It also follows that this is a field where a substantial body of 'human rights' literature exists (Thorold, 1996; Clements, 1999a; Fennell, 1999), and for this reason, the following analysis is necessarily brief.

In *Winterwerp v the Netherlands* (1979)[78], and a series of subsequent cases[79], the Court laid down a number of factors which must be satisfied before the detention of a person of unsound mind satisfies the requirements of Article 5(1)(e) including:

1. The mental disorder must be reliably established by objective medical expertise.

2. The nature or degree of the disorder must be sufficiently extreme to justify the detention.

3. The detention should only last as long as the medical disorder (and its required severity) persists.

4. If the detention is potentially indefinite, then there must be a system of periodic reviews by a tribunal that has power to discharge.

5. The detention must be in a hospital, clinic or other appropriate institution authorised for the detention of such persons[80].

In addition, Article 5(4) directs that all detained patients must have the right to apply to a tribunal (the Mental Health Review Tribunal in England and Wales) to challenge the legality of their detention; and the tribunal is required to make such determinations 'speedily' and to have the power to order the patient's release where it considers it appropriate.

There have been many cases in which the precise meaning of most of these provisions have been clarified. For instance, that a routine delay of eight weeks in convening a tribunal hearing violates the 'speedily' requirement[81]; that it is for the state to prove the existence of a mental disorder, not the patient to disprove it[82]; that the tribunal will not be sufficiently independent if one of its members makes it clear that he has prejudged the outcome[83], and once a person ceases to have a mental disorder, then the detention ceases to be lawful[84].

Loss of liberty

One of the remaining uncertainties relates to the precise meaning of 'detention'. Once a person is detained, then all the rights under Article 5 apply. Clearly this occurs when a person is formally arrested by a police officer or sectioned under the 1983 Mental Health Act. What however is the situation of persons who are in psychiatric wards but have not been sectioned, but lack the mental capacity to ask to leave; or of frail elderly patients in long-stay wards or units where the doors are secured with 'confusional handles' or even locked. Are these people 'detained'? If they are, then they should have the detailed procedural rights under Article 5. At present there is no definitive answer to this question.

HM v Switzerland (2002)[85] concerned the forcible removal of the 84-year-old complainant to a care home. The municipal authorities had received many complaints from neighbours and statutory agencies concerned about her self–neglect and increasing frailty. She was not able to feed or even dress herself without assistance (which she lacked), and spent most of her time lying in bed. Informal attempts to resolve this problem had failed because, the municipality alleged, of her obstructive behaviour. She was, accordingly, moved to a care home against her wishes. Although not actually under lock and key, and although able to maintain personal contacts, write letters and telephone the outside world, it was clear that she was not permitted to leave and that if she did, she would be brought back to the home. Regrettably, the majority of the Court (five of the seven judges) concluded that she was not 'detained' and therefore had no rights under Article 5 of the Convention. Two of the judges however forcefully rejected this view.

The issue is of importance, because many disabled people, particularly older people with dementia, find themselves in not dissimilar situations. If they are 'detained' then they have substantial rights and safeguards under Article 5; if not, then they have no such protection. The Swiss case can be contrasted with the House of Lords' decision of *R v Bournewood Community and Mental Health Trust ex parte L* (1998)[86]. This is a pre-1998 Human Rights Act case that has attracted substantial comment (from for example, Howard, 1998; Mahendra, 1998; Dawson, 1999; Dickenson and Shah, 1999; Glover, 1999), and which is presently awaiting determination by the European Court of Human Rights.

Bournewood, as it has become known, concerns 'L', who at the time was aged 48. L has autism and he lacks the ability to communicate consent or dissent to treatment, or express a preference as to where he should live. He requires 24-hour care, sometimes injures himself, and pushes others, and every few days his behaviour becomes particularly difficult to manage. Since the age of 15, L had been a long-term resident at the Bournewood Hospital. However, when aged 45 he went to live with Mr and Mrs E who took responsibility for his care and regarded him as 'one of the family'. Despite his periodic outbursts they cared for him for over three years without need to call for the assistance of the police or the hospital. However, in 1997, while at a Day Centre, he had a challenging episode and because his carers could not be contacted he was taken to the Bournewood Hospital and sedated. When his carers went to collect L and return him home, the psychiatrist explained that it had been decided that L should remain in the unit for a further period of time, and that they could not see L because it might upset him and make him want to return home with them. L had not, however, been formally detained, as he was 'quite compliant' and had not objected to remaining in the unit.

There was no consensus among the judges hearing the case as to whether L was in fact 'detained', and this will be a key question if and when it is finally heard by the Strasbourg Court. Lord Steyn listed the following factors as relevant to the question: (1) L was sedated and physically carried to the hospital; (2) the admission by the psychiatrist that had he resisted he would have been sectioned; (3) he was regularly sedated to ensure that he remained 'tractable'; (4) visits by the carers were vetoed; and (5) although not in a locked ward, he was kept under continuous observation. Having regard to all these factors, Lord Steyn concluded, "the suggestion that L was free to go is a fairy tale" and he expressed concern that patients such as L could be detained without any of the safeguards provided by the 1983 Mental Health Act – describing this as "an indefensible gap in our mental health law".

If the European Court of Human Rights conclude that L was detained, this is likely to have a major impact on the procedures applied when compliant mental health service users are accommodated in hospitals and care homes, for at present only a small fraction of them are detained under the provisions of the 1983 Mental Health Act[87]. One consequence could be that they would be entitled to claim compensation for their unlawful detention (Article 5(5)). The government has conceded that action needs to be taken to address the so-called 'Bournewood gap' and Part 5 of its draft Mental Health Bill (DoH, 2002a) introduces "a range of safeguards to guard against possible inappropriate treatment or detention" of "incapacitated patients who do not resist" (DoH, 2002b, para 187).

As noted in Chapter 1, a separate and anachronistic power to detain chronically sick, disabled or elderly persons exists under Section 47 1948 National Assistance Act[88]. The provision authorises a removal order to be made, where the Community physician has certified that a person "suffering from grave, chronic disease or being aged, infirm or physically incapacitated is living in unsanitary conditions" and is "unable to devote to himself and is not receiving from other persons proper care and attention". Inappropriate use of the provision has the clear potential to violate the Convention. Its scope extends well beyond the categories of persons specified in Article 5(1)(e) and it permits removal for up to three weeks on the authority of only the most limited of medical evidence without the respondent having any prior notice of the application or right to be heard. The certifying doctors need have no particular knowledge of the detained person.

Private and family life and the home

The scope of the rights

Article 8 is the main vehicle by which the Convention seeks to promote respect for every individual's privacy, family life and home. That this has proved to be the most dynamic and adaptable of the Convention rights is perhaps unsurprising given that it seeks to hold the ring between the competing interests of private individuals in their relations with each other, and with the state. Just as with all the 'qualified' Convention rights, it is founded on the premise of pluralism, tolerance and broadmindedness[89]; a provocative combination that inevitably becomes the punchbag for controversial disputes concerning, for instance, the right of gay men or gypsies, or indeed disabled people, to an equality of opportunity in our imperfect civil society.

While 'family life' and 'the home' have, in large measure, been given their everyday meanings, the concept of 'private life' has acquired an altogether more expansive interpretation, including a "person's physical and psychological integrity" for which respect is due in order to "ensure the development, without outside interference, of the personality of each individual in his relations with other human beings"[90]. The Court has reworked this formula to fit various situations. Thus in *Mikulic v Croatia* (2002)[91] (a case concerning the applicant's wish to establish the identity of her father) it held that private life embraced "aspects of an individual's physical and social identity" including a "right to establish relationships with other human beings".

Family life

In Chapter 3 we have highlighted the extent to which disabled children have been separated from their parents and disabled parents from their children. *Kutzner v Germany* (2002)[92] is an example of the latter. The applicants' five- and seven-year-old daughters had been removed from their care because it was alleged that the parents' 'impaired mental development' rendered them incapable of bringing up their children. There was no suggestion however of any neglect or ill-treatment. The children were separated from each other and eventually fostered. For the first six months they had no contact with their parents and thereafter it was restricted to one hour monthly.

A number of experts, during the German proceedings, challenged the intervention by the social services agency, stressing the great benefits derived by the children from their relationship with their parents, and argued that they were capable of raising their children equally as well in emotional as intellectual terms – subject to the provision by the authorities of extra educational support for the children.

In finding a violation of the family's rights under Article 8, the Court referred to the state's positive obligation in such cases to take measures to facilitate the family's reunion, as soon as practically possible; it considered that these included the provision of additional educational, and other measures, to support the family. The Article 8 violation related not only to the original removal of the children, by their separation while in care, but also to the restrictions upon parental and sibling contact[93].

The Kutzner complaint is noteworthy as the first Court judgment concerning the obligations upon the state to provide support to disabled parents in order to maintain their right to a 'family life'. Of concern, however, is the absence of any equivalent decisions (or, it appears, complaints) concerning the rights of disabled children. As research suggests that the acts and omissions of the state cause substantial disruption to the family lives of disabled children, the absence of Strasbourg complaints is almost certainly attributable to the double discrimination they face in accessing justice – as children and as disabled people.

Private life

As noted above, the concept of 'private life' has been given a particularly expansive interpretation by the European Court of Human Rights, and some aspects of this approach are considered separately below.

Sexual rights

The absence of complaints by disabled people challenging the state-imposed restrictions on their sexual freedoms, would appear to be explained by the 'access to justice' barriers discussed above, rather than this issue being of no concern to them (Shakespeare, 1996). This absence can be contrasted with the large numbers of complaints received by transsexual, gay and lesbian people. Indeed, as we have noted in Chapter 1, the Home Office has accepted that "the present proscription of all sexual activity with those with severe learning disabilities ... may constitute a breach of Article 8" (Home Office, 2000, para 11, app H6).

The Court and Commission require strict justification from states in respect of any restrictions that are placed upon individual sexual freedom "given that it impinges on a most intimate aspect of affected individuals' private lives"[94]. In view of this, the Law Commission (Law Commission, 2000, para 4.27) suggested that the present broad approach would almost certainly fail the Strasbourg test, commenting:

> ... what is it that this vulnerable category of people needs to be protected from? A sexual relationship between a person of full mental capability and one with severe learning disabilities may well involve an element of abuse that the criminal law should proscribe, particularly where there is a 'care' relationship. A sexual relationship between two people, both of whom have such disabilities, may not intrinsically involve any abuse – although, depending upon the circumstances, a particular relationship might be abusive. (Sinason, 1992, para 427)

The right to marry and found a family

Allied to the question of sexual rights of disabled people is the Article 12 right, namely "men and women of marriageable age have the right to marry and to found a family, according to the national laws governing the exercise of this right". Although the Convention permits procedural restrictions on the right to marry, the Court has held that these "must not restrict or reduce the right in such a way or to such an extent that the very essence of the right is impaired"[95].

In order to enter into a marriage contract, UK law requires that the parties have sufficient mental capacity to understand the consequent responsibilities, but it has been held not to require "a high degree of intelligence"[96]. It appears unlikely therefore that domestic legislation is in breach of this limb of Article 12; particularly since the 1983 Marriage Act makes special provision for the marriage of persons housebound or detained under the 1983 Mental Health Act.

As to the second limb – the right to found a family – this clearly has implications in relation to the extent of the positive obligation on the state to provide services and other assistance in order to make this right (and the associated right to a family life under Article 8) a reality. The government has however accepted the importance of the provision of support of disabled adults in their parenting role (Goodinge, 2000), and in the context of parents with learning disabilities committed itself to ensuring such help is made available (DoH, 2001). Against this backdrop, and the requirement in Section 17(1) of the 1989 Children Act to provide support and services, to promote the upbringing of such children by their families, it appears likely that recourse to the Convention in domestic proceedings should be unnecessary, for the pre-existing obligations on authorities are directed towards the same goal.

Personal integrity and physical barriers

As noted above, the Court has progressively expanded its interpretation of the meaning of 'private life' within the context of Article 8. In *Botta v Italy* (1998)[97], a physically disabled applicant, sought to take it further, by complaining that physical barriers stopped him gaining access to Italian beaches, and as a consequence this amounted to a violation of his rights under Article 8, since it rendered him "unable to enjoy a normal social life which would enable him to participate in the life of the community".

The Court noted that:

> While the essential object of Article 8 is to protect the individual against arbitrary interference by the public authorities, it does not merely compel the state to abstain from such interference: in addition to this negative undertaking, there may be positive obligations inherent in effective respect for private or family life. These obligations may involve the adoption of measures designed to secure respect for private life even in the sphere of the relations of individuals between themselves.

Having determined that a failure to remove barriers could, in certain situations, place a state in breach of its Article 8 responsibilities, the Court decided that the extent of this obligation depended upon whether a "direct and immediate link" could be established between "the measures sought by an applicant and the latter's private and/or family life". In effect, the question to ask was 'How severe were the consequences of the state's inaction for Mr Botta?' It then considered those cases where it had found there to be a positive obligation under Article 8. These included situations where applicants were at risk of abuse[98], illness[99] and (in the case of *X and Y v Netherlands* [1985][100]) a rape going unpunished.

By this measure, the Court considered that the Botta complaint failed:

> In the instant case, however, the right asserted by Mr Botta, namely the right to gain access to the beach and the sea at a place distant from his normal place of residence during his holidays, concerns interpersonal relations of such broad and indeterminate scope that there can be no conceivable direct link between the measures the State was urged to take in order to make good the omissions of the private bathing establishments and the applicant's private life.

The judgment is important since the Court accepted that unreasonable barriers (physical or otherwise) might violate a disabled person's rights under Article 8. In each case an assessment will be required, establishing whether the consequences for the applicant are so serious as to invoke a positive obligation on the state to take remedial action. Although in many situations the 1995 Disability Discrimination Act duties will provide a more direct remedy, Article 8 will be relevant in those situations where the discrimination does not come within the ambit of the 1995 Act (that is, where it could not be construed as relating to 'goods or services'). Much of the argument in Botta is, however, reducible to the language of the 1995 Act – in terms of a failure to 'make reasonable adjustments' having a 'substantial adverse effect' on the disabled person.

Privacy and confidential information

The state holds particularly sensitive confidential information about many disabled people; for instance personal histories, medical records, medical photographs and so on. It also holds copious quantities of information about the dangers posed by certain treatments, activities, environmental risks and so on. Article 8 contains a presumption against disclosure of the former and in favour of disclosure of the latter[101].

Although the Convention's approach to the question of the confidentiality of personal information has an "additional dimension to that of our common law", they both "require that a balance be struck between the various interests involved"[102] and commence from a presumption against disclosure to third parties[103]. In *Z v Finland* (1998)[104] for instance (a case concerning the disclosure by a court of the fact that the complainant was HIV positive), it was held that:

> ... the protection of personal data, not least medical data, is of fundamental importance to a person's enjoyment of his or her right to respect for private and family life as guaranteed by Article 8 of the Convention (Article 8). Respecting the confidentiality of health data is a vital principle in the legal systems of all the Contracting Parties to the Convention. It is crucial not

only to respect the sense of privacy of a patient but also to preserve his or her confidence in the medical profession and in the health services in general.

In *JT v UK* (1998)[105] the Commission concluded that the automatic disclosure of personal information about a patient detained under the 1983 Mental Health Act to her 'nearest relative', constituted an unreasonable interference with her rights under Article 8. What was fundamentally wrong with the process was not that disclosure could occur, but that it was automatic; that there was no provision for balancing the competing interests for and against disclosure. The appropriate approach to the 'balancing' decision (particularly when the relevant person lacks the necessary mental capacity to agree or object to the disclosure to a third party), has now been reviewed by the Court of Appeal[106] to bring it into line with the Strasbourg requirements. In relation to the specific problem of disclosure to 'nearest relatives', the government has tabled proposals to amend the 1983 Act (DoH, 2000a, Part 7).

In *Gaskin v UK* (1989)[107] what was in issue was the extent of the complainant's right to see his own social services file. He had been in local authority care since a young age and on achieving his majority wanted to read the full file so as to discover about his past, how he came into care and other relevant information. The Court accordingly held that the records contained in the file related to his private and family life and therefore engaged the obligations under Article 8. Unfortunately UK law, as it applied at that time, did not allow him access to information on the file that had been contributed by third parties (without the third parties' actual consent to disclosure). The Court held that such an approach was 'disproportionate', stating:

> ... persons in the situation of the applicant have a vital interest, protected by the Convention, in receiving the information necessary to know and to understand their childhood and early development. On the other hand, it must be borne in mind that confidentiality of public records is of importance for receiving objective and reliable information, and that such confidentiality can also be necessary for the protection of third persons. Under the latter aspect, a system like the British one, which makes access to records dependent on the consent of the contributor, can in principle be considered to be compatible with the obligations under Article 8 ... [but only] if it provides that an independent authority finally decides whether access has to be granted in cases where a contributor fails to answer or withholds consent. No such procedure was available to the applicant in the present case.

As a result of the judgment, the 1998 Data Protection Act amended the law, so as to provide for such an independent arbiter (that is, the court or the Data Protection Commissioner).

Home

The fundamental importance of adequate housing for disabled people has been repeatedly emphasised (for example, Arnold, 1993; Audit Commission, 1998; Oldman and Beresford, 1998), as has the Strasbourg Court's assertion that the right protected by Article 8 is the right to respect for one's existing home[108], and not a right to be provided with housing accommodation. However, the Court's approach appears to be changing and is subject to a number of qualifications, most notably that expressed in *Marzari v Italy* (1999)[109]. The *Marzari* complaint concerned a complicated and long running dispute between the applicant and his local authority relating to his need for specially adapted housing (arising out of his seriously disabling illness, metabolic myopathy). The applicant had been evicted from his apartment for refusal to pay his rent and he had refused alternative accommodation which he considered inadequate. While the Court declared the complaint inadmissible, it did, however, make the following important point:

> ... although Article 8 does not guarantee the right to have one's housing problem solved by the authorities, a refusal of the authorities to provide assistance in this respect to an individual suffering from a severe disease might in certain circumstances raise an issue under Article 8 of the Convention because of the impact of such a refusal on the private life of the individual.

This observation by the Court would appear to carry the additional implication that any accommodation so provided by the state would have to be suitable for the disabled person's particular needs – or at the very least 'fit for habitation'. Support for this approach comes from a recent Court of Appeal decision where, although it held that houses let with condensation/mildew/mould and unfit for habitation did not violate the tenant's rights under Article 8, it left open the possibility that in different circumstances a violation could arise[110].

Institutional accommodation

For many disabled people, their home is (in one form or another) in an institutional setting. Provided the stay has been for a reasonable length of time[111], the care home or hospital ward, for example, will be deemed the person's 'home' for the purposes of Article 8. Accordingly, any attempt to move the resident, will have to be justified as being proportional. *R v North and East Devon Health Authority ex parte Coughlan* (1999)[112] concerned an attempt by a health authority to move the applicant from her specialist NHS unit where she had lived for six years. Having regard to all the circumstances (which included the health authority's desire to close the facility for budgetary reasons) the Court considered that the authority had failed to establish that such an interference with the applicant's Article 8 right was justified.

In relation to the placement of disabled people in an institutional setting, there is an additional issue under the Convention, namely, whether this could constitute discriminatory action (that is, contrary to Article 8 in combination with Article 14). Although no such domestic or European challenge has been mounted, there is relevant authority for this proposition in the form of a US Supreme Court decision, *Olmstead v LC* (1999)[113]. The Olmstead judgment concerned the State of Georgia, which skewed its funding arrangements to favour institutional placements, rather than community-based independent living placements. The applicants alleged that this constituted unlawful discrimination and the majority of the Supreme Court agreed. While the Court emphasised that the financial resources of states were relevant factors in determining their policies, it stressed the importance of policies being rational and fair, and of the basic principle that 'unnecessary institutionalisation' should be avoided if possible. In the view of the majority:

> The identification of unjustified segregation as discrimination reflects two evident judgments. Institutional placement of persons who can handle and benefit from community settings perpetuates unwarranted assumptions that persons so isolated are incapable or unworthy of participating in community life ....

and

> ... confinement in an institution severely diminishes the everyday life activities of individuals, including family relations, social contacts, work options, economic independence, educational advancement, and cultural enrichment.

Governmental policies in the UK have consistently skewed funding towards institutional care. The Audit Commission (1996) for instance, has commented:

> The financial incentive for authorities to use residential care remains strong. In nearly all situations it is substantially cheaper for local authorities to place people in residential care, even where there is no difference between the gross cost of residential care and care at home. (p 26)

The government has also conceded that certain Income Support arrangements, now partially phased out, have favoured placements in residential homes over maintaining people in their own homes (DoH, 1998, para 7.25; Royal Commission on Long-Term Care, 1999, para 4.28). It follows that central government policies, as well as those implemented by health authorities and local authorities, may be amenable to challenge under the principle of "unnecessary, or indeed, disproportionate institutionalisation"[114].

Property and possessions

As has been noted in Chapter 2, the right under Article 1 of the First Protocol "to the peaceful enjoyment of his possessions" is so widely drawn, and permits so many exceptions, that violations are seldom found. However any disputed interference with a possession, which may include social security income, will generally have to be justified at a fair hearing. Unfair interferences therefore may result in collateral challenges under Articles 6(1) and 14. An example of possible Article 6(1) violations relate to the discretionary process for challenging appointeeship orders (noted above), and the absence of legal aid in proceedings before the Court of Protection. An example of a discriminatory interference with property rights is provided by *McGregor v UK* (1997)[115]. The applicant worked as a veterinary nurse and cared for her husband, a disabled person. Her application for a special tax allowance was refused on the ground that it was only available for working men with 'incapacitated' wives and not vice versa. Her complaint was upheld by the Commission on the basis that it amounted to a discriminatory violation of her property rights (that is, she paid more money in tax because she was a woman).

Education and segregation

As noted in Chapter 2, the right to education under Article 2 of the First Protocol is phrased in negative terms, namely "no person shall be denied the right to education". However the Court considers that a number of positive obligations accompany this right, and of particular relevance in the present context it has isolated two principles of importance[116]:

1. Although the Article does not specify the language in which education must be conducted "the right to education would be meaningless if it did not imply in favour of its beneficiaries, the right to be educated in the national language or in one of the national languages, as the case may be".
2. For the 'right to education' to be effective, it is necessary that, "the individual who is the beneficiary should have the possibility of drawing profit from the education received, that is to say, the right to obtain, in conformity with the rules in force in each state, and in one form or another, official recognition of the studies which he has completed".

For some disabled children the issue of language is relevant, and not one of choice (for example, in relation to the use of sign language or requiring of specific forms of speech and language therapy assistance). Although, as stated by the Court there is no general right to be educated in any particular language, the content of the education provided must be capable of being communicated in some effective way; otherwise it would be 'meaningless' – and with no prospect of "drawing profit from the education received". It would appear to follow that the First Protocol right demands that reasonable measures are taken to ensure that appropriate language assistance is available.

The government has also accepted that the right to education includes the right of access to existing state educational institutions, but has successfully argued that this is not an absolute right, and does not require access to be made available to every classroom[117].

A number of complaints[118] by parents of disabled children have been considered by the Commission concerning the second limb of the Article 2 right, namely that the obligation on the state to respect the "right of parents to ensure [that state provided] education and teaching in conformity with their own religious and philosophical convictions". In each case it was argued that the state's refusal to agree to their children being educated in 'mainstream' schools amounted to a lack of respect for their philosophical convictions and unreasonable discrimination (contrary to Article 14). Such complaints have not managed, so far, to get beyond the following formulaic response:

> The Commission observes that there is an increasing body of opinion which holds that, whenever possible, disabled children should be brought up with normal children of their own age. The Commission recognises, however, that this policy cannot apply to all handicapped children. It further recognises that there must be a wide measure of discretion left to the appropriate authorities as to how to make the best use possible of the resources available to them in the interests of disabled children generally. While these authorities must place weight on parental convictions, it cannot be said that the second sentence of Article 2 requires the placing of a child with severe learning difficulties in a general school (with the expense of additional teaching staff which would be needed) rather than in an available place in a special school.

Although social attitudes and state arrangements for the education of disabled children are constantly changing, it may be that the Strasbourg Court's development of its interpretation of the Article 2/Protocol I right will prove to be of little value in the UK. This is because the positive obligations created by our domestic special educational needs legislation (including the recent enhancement via the 2001 Special Needs and Disability Act), and the more robust approach to the issue of 'resources' by our courts[119] provides an entitlement, however inadequate, well in advance of that presently envisaged by Strasbourg.

Thought expression and association

Thought, conscience and religion

The Article 9 right to freedom of thought, conscience and religion has two aspects. The right to hold such opinions is absolute, but the right to communicate them, or to 'proselytise', is subject to the familiar proportionality restrictions.

No disabled people have made complaints under this provision, which has largely been the preserve of religious organisations. However, coercive action against the parents of a disabled child could give rise to complaints. By way of example, in *Hoffman v Austria* (1996)[120], a violation was found in relation to an order depriving a mother of the custody of her children on the grounds that she was a Jehovah's Witness. Potentially therefore issues such as the furore over the decision by deaf parents who took deliberate positive action to ensure that they conceived a deaf baby, (Winterson, 2002) – including criticisms that they had "violated the sacred duty of parenthood" (Teather, 2002) – may well have fallen to be considered under this Article had for instance, the media condemnation resulted in a prohibitive legislative response.

Expression

As noted in Chapter 2, Article 10 of the Convention protects not only the right to freedom of expression, but also the freedom to receive and impart information. In relation to this ancillary obligation, the Court has mainly been concerned with cases that engage the right to receive information, and in this respect the Article 10 right was largely sidelined by the developing jurisprudence of Article 8 (as noted above) concerning the right of access to information of importance to one's private life.

Two aspects of the Article 10 right appear to be of particular relevance to disabled people:

- the extent to which the right to 'receive information' can be considered as embodying a positive obligation on the state to ensure that information is expressed in a medium intelligible to people with sensory impairments or learning disabilities; and
- the extent to which the right to 'impart' information embodies a similar positive component, namely the obligation on the state to provide assistance to enable disabled people with communication difficulties to express themselves.

On the basis of the Court's present approach, the answer to both is probably that any positive obligation is minimal. In *Guerra v Italy* (1998)[121] (a case concerning severe environmental risks from a chemical factory), the applicants argued that Article 10:

> ... imposed on States not just a duty to make available information to the public on environmental matters ... but also a positive obligation to collect, process and disseminate such information, which by its nature could not otherwise come to the knowledge of the public.

The Court (having found a violation of Article 8) adopted a restrictive approach to the Article 10 right, stating:

> ... that freedom to receive information, referred to in paragraph 2 of Article 10 of the Convention, 'basically prohibits a government from restricting a person from receiving information that others wish or may be willing to impart to him'[122].... That freedom cannot be construed as imposing on a State, in circumstances such as those of the present case, positive obligations to collect and disseminate information of its own motion.

In so deciding, the Court held to the same line it had followed in response to an earlier complaint concerning access to police records, where it had again ruled out any positive obligation under Article 10, ruling that it "does not embody an obligation on the Government to impart such information to the individual"[123].

It appears unlikely, therefore, that the Strasbourg Court is prepared to see Article 10 used as a vehicle for the provision of assistance and services for disabled people who have communication and/or comprehension difficulties. Given the Court's willingness to develop Article 8 to encompass all aspects of a person's 'physical and psychological integrity' (as reviewed above), it may be that questions concerning the provision of speech and language therapy services, advocacy and other assistance will more naturally fall to be considered in the context of that Article.

It does not, however, appear inappropriate to use the language of 'human rights' when discussing the provision of services to assist communication and/or comprehension. The Department of Health itself has quoted the following extract with approval (DoH, 2000, para 3.125): "disabled children have the human right to take part in play and leisure activities and to freely express themselves" (Morris, 1998, p 20).

Voting and election rights

A particular aspect of expression is of course the right to participate in free and fair elections; a right protected by Article 3 of the First Protocol. Although the Court has held that the right embodies "the principle of equality of treatment of all citizens in the exercise of their right to vote and their right to stand for election"[124], it remains the case that many disabled people experience problems exercising this right. At the 2001 General Election, for instance, it is estimated that almost 70% of polling stations had significant accessibility problems (Scott and Morris, 2001).

Since the right only applies to the election of the 'legislature' and has been broadly interpreted by the Court to permit significant restrictions by the state, it appears that domestic law will prove to be of greater practical relevance. In this respect, as a result of concern about the disenfranchisement of certain patients in psychiatric hospitals (Parker, 1996) and the inaccessibility of polling stations/polling information (Enticott et al, 1992) amendments have been made to the 1983 Representation of the People Act[125].

Association

As we have noted in Chapter 3, research highlights the isolated, and 'friendless' experiences of many disabled people frequently dislocated from family and community (Humphries and Gordon, 1992; Smith, 1994; Morris, 1995; French, 1996; Gordon et al, 2000).

Although (as we noted in Chapter 2), Article 11 addresses the issue of association, the Court has held the right to be qualified by the subsequent clause: "including the right to form and to join trade unions for the protection of his interests". It has consistently rejected interpretations that would have the right to 'associate' mean 'share the company of'. In a 1981 complaint, prisoners at the Maze prison in Northern Ireland alleged that their segregation and solitary confinement amounted to "an unjustifiable infringement of their freedom of association with others". Rejecting this construction the Court stated[126]:

> As the language of Article 11 suggests, the concept of freedom of association, of which the right to form and join trade unions is a special aspect, is concerned with the right to form or be affiliated with a group or organisation pursuing particular aims. It does not concern the right of prisoners to share the company of other prisoners or to 'associate' with other prisoners in this sense.

Yet again it appears that Article 8 may prove to be the more effective right. Given that the concept of 'private life' has been applied by the Court in the context of "the development ... of the personality of each individual in his relations with other human beings"[127], it is a relatively small step to link this with the social isolation and segregation experienced by many disabled people.

Discrimination

Article 14, the main non-discrimination Article within the Convention, is an imperfect provision: evidenced not least by the rarity with which it is found to have been violated. Although the problems with the Article stem in part from its scope[128], the main cause has undoubtedly been the hesitancy with which it has been applied by the Strasbourg Court (a hesitancy that need not necessarily be followed by our domestic judges). The frustration felt by many with this approach was recently vented by one of the Strasbourg judges, Judge Bonello, when in a dissenting opinion in a race discrimination complaint[129] he stated:

> I consider it particularly disturbing that the Court, in over fifty years of pertinacious judicial scrutiny, has not, to date, found one single instance of violation of the right to life (Article 2) or the right not to be subjected to torture or other degrading or inhuman treatment or punishment (Article 3)

induced by the race, colour or place of origin of the victim. Leafing through the annals of the Court, an uninformed observer would be justified to conclude that, for over fifty years democratic Europe has been exempted from any suspicion of racism, intolerance or xenophobia. The Europe projected by the Court's case-law is that of an exemplary haven of ethnic fraternity, in which peoples of the most diverse origin coalesce without distress, prejudice or recrimination.

Judge Bonello's complaint rings equally true if applied in the context of disability discrimination. Article 14 requires that the "enjoyment of the rights and freedoms set forth in this Convention shall be secured without discrimination on any ground such as sex, race, colour, language, religion, political or other opinion, national or social origin, association with a national minority, property, birth or other status". The problem with this wording stems from the limitation of the right to 'Convention rights'. This means that Article 14 is not free-standing. A complaint alleging discriminatory treatment must also establish that this concerned a Convention right. Thus in *MacGregor v UK* (1997) (discussed above) the complaint concerned sex discrimination in relation to her possessions (that is, Article 1 of the First Protocol). A difference in treatment in relation to a non-Convention right (for instance in the allocation of council housing) would not violate Article 14[130].

It follows that wherever there is a choice between using its protection or that afforded by the 1995 Disability Discrimination Act, the 1995 Act will almost always be the better provision. The usefulness of Article 14 however lies in its far wider coverage and in its being in no way constrained by the technical restrictions evident in the 1995 legislation (that is, those present in Part I of the Act).

Although 'disability' is not included within Article 14's illustrative list of grounds upon which unreasonable discrimination is not permitted, it is generally considered that it would constitute a 'status' attracting its protection. This has yet to be determined (since no finding of an Article 14 violation on grounds of disability has yet occurred). Indeed, in *McIntyre v UK* (1995)[131] (a case concerning alleged education discrimination), the government refused to accept that disability was a 'status' that came within the protection of Article 14. However, since the case was inadmissible on other grounds, the Commission found it unnecessary to rule on this question.

The Court applies a number of principles in cases where a violation of Article 14 is alleged. In many respects these mirror the more rigid principles found within the 1995 Disability Discrimination Act. The Strasbourg principles require:

- evidence of a difference of treatment (generally by reference to an appropriate comparator to whom the condition does not apply);
- that the treatment relates to a Convention right;

- that any difference of treatment must pursue a legitimate aim and be proportionate[132]. However in this respect, unlike the 1995 Disability Discrimination Act there is no exhaustive list of grounds for 'justification' or guidance on what would be a reasonable adjustment and so on.

Indirect discrimination

Although the Court has not directly acknowledged the concept of 'indirect discrimination', increasingly its decisions are making this principle part of the Strasbourg jurisprudence. The first significant recognition of this approach came in *Thlimmenos v Greece* (2000)[133] where the Court held that unlawful discrimination can occur where a state applies the same sanctions against people in materially different situations – as opposed to a failure to treat similar people in a similar way. Thlimmenos concerned a person who had served a term of imprisonment for refusing military service on religious grounds. He was subsequently barred from becoming a chartered accountant because of this criminal conviction. The Court held that this action failed to distinguish between people who had convictions due to dishonesty from those who had convictions for religious or other conscientious reasons and was in violation of Article 14. Its judgment includes:

> The Court has so far considered that the right under Article 14 not to be discriminated against in the enjoyment of the rights guaranteed under the Convention is violated when States treat differently persons in analogous situations without providing an objective and reasonable justification.... However, the Court considers that this is not the only facet of the prohibition of discrimination in Article 14. The right not to be discriminated against in the enjoyment of the rights guaranteed under the Convention is also violated when States without an objective and reasonable justification fail to treat differently persons whose situations are significantly different.

The above extract was specifically referred to by Judge Greve in his separate opinion in the complaint of *Price v UK* (2001)[134] (which concerned the imprisonment of the Thalidomide impaired applicant (considered above). Although the case was not considered in the context of Article 14 (since a straightforward violation of Article 3 was found), there seems little doubt that the Court would also have been prepared to find a violation of Article 14 in this case by virtue of the failure to treat her differently from other prisoners.

The issue of resources

The issue of positive obligations has dominated this chapter's review of the Convention's relevance to the experiences of disabled people. The delivery of these obligations is, to a greater or lesser degree, resource-dependent. In general judges are wary of cases with significant resource implications, believing such questions are better decided by parliament.

Reference has already been made to the judgment in *R v Cambridge Health Authority ex parte B* (1995)[135], where the Court of Appeal referred to the "difficult and agonising judgments" that had to be made "as to how a limited budget is best allocated" and concluded that these judgments were for health authorities, not courts. Lord Hoffman, a senior Law Lord put the position frankly in his Commercial Bar (COMBAR) 2001 lecture (Hoffman, 2001)[136]:

> ... even when a case appears to involve no more than the construction of a statute or interpretation of a common law rule, the courts are very circumspect about giving an answer which would materially affect the distribution of public expenditure.

His views have been echoed by many of his colleagues; recently Lord Nicholls in *Re S and W (children: care plan)* (2002)[137] explained why he considered it inappropriate for the House of Lords to extend its power to supervise social services child protection arrangements, stating:

> It would have far-reaching practical ramifications for local authorities and their care of children.... It would be likely to have a material effect on authorities' allocation of scarce financial and other resources. This in turn would affect authorities' discharge of their responsibilities to other children.... These are matters for decision by Parliament, not the courts....

It is not only British courts that consider resource-dependent decisions to be better suited to political rather than judicial determination. From the US[138] to New Zealand[139], and from India[140] to Strasbourg[141], courts have grappled with the 'resource question' and admitted to caution when being invited to expansively interpret a provision with the effect of creating a new positive obligation on the state. A recent example of the South African Constitutional Court, in relation to a health treatment decision, included the following[142]:

> The provincial administration which is responsible for health services in Kwa-Zulu–Natal has to make decisions about the funding that should be made available for health care and how such funds should be spent. These choices involve difficult decisions to be taken at the political level in fixing the health budget, and at the functional level in deciding upon the priorities to be met. A court will be slow to interfere with rational decisions taken in good faith by the political organs and medical authorities whose responsibility it is to deal with such matters.

However, if the Court's role is merely 'interpretive', why should judges be shy of interpreting, in a positive way, a right created by parliament, in the clear knowledge that it would demand significant resources? This indeed was the situation that confronted our domestic courts in the case of *R v Gloucestershire County Council ex parte Barry* (1997)[143]. Parliament had legislated via the 1970 Chronically Sick and Disabled Persons Act to provide specific rights for disabled people in the full knowledge that it would be expensive[144]. Over the years, however it failed to adequately resource the Act and in 1997 the courts had to determine whether an authority could plead poverty as a way of avoiding its obligations. A number of senior judges considered the situation straightforward. Sir John Balcombe, for instance, observed that "Parliament knows very well how to confer a power, which will enable resources to be taken into account; if it uses language apt to impose a duty it presumably means what it says"[145]. In similar vein, Lord Lloyd in his dissenting speech commented that the "passing of the 1970 Chronically Sick and Disabled Persons Act was a noble aspiration. Having willed the end, Parliament must be asked to provide the means"[146]. Ultimately, however, the House of Lords interpreted the legislation so as to allow resource considerations, and thereby allowed local authorities to "escape their impossible position"[147].

The reticence of courts when faced with resource-dependent legislation cannot always be interpreted as deference to parliament: reticence in such situations can be overtly political – in effect the court assuming the role of a conservative (small 'c') third chamber of the legislature. Arguably this is what occurred in the *Gloucestershire* judgment. For there is nothing intrinsically unjusticiable about laws that place financial responsibilities upon individuals or state bodies, even if those laws relate to 'human rights' as opposed to the regulation of property interests. As James Harris (2002) has observed, in his critique of Nozick's attack on the concept of positive obligations (Nozick, 1974, p 119), "Nor do the social conventions under-pinning property institutions crystallise in such a way that every resource-holding is immutable and morally sacrosanct. Rather, both juristic doctrine and wider social conventions about property-allocations are constantly in flux".

Non-resource dependent positive rights

Notwithstanding judicial caution in the face of the 'resource argument', certain rights have been held to transcend its perplexing rhetoric. As this review discloses, our domestic courts effectively recognise a core set of irreducible positive healthcare obligations – positive rights to healthcare in respect of which "it is not legitimate ... to take into account the wider practical issues as to allocation of limited financial resources"[148].

Beyond the realm of healthcare, certain other fundamental and 'absolute' rights also appear immune to resource arguments. As we have noted, in *R v Gloucestershire County Council ex parte Mahfood* (1995)[149], McCowan LJ held that budgetary difficulties could not excuse a failure to provide social care where "persons would be at severe physical risk if they were unable to have [such services]". Using the language of the Convention he was, in effect, stating that limited resources could not be used as a reason for allowing a violation of Article 3 to take place.

The same must also be true of Article 5. It is difficult to conceive of a situation where a shortage of financial resources alone, could be seen as a valid argument for keeping someone detained. *R v Manchester City Council ex parte Stennett* (2002)[150] concerned the right of detained patients to 'free' aftercare services under Section 117 of the 1983 Mental Health Act. The court accepted that in many cases patients were only discharged from their detention in psychiatric wards if they 'agreed' to move into a specialist care home. It was argued, therefore that to require payment for this service would, in effect be requiring a patient to pay for his or her freedom. Lord Steyn found such a proposition compelling, stating:

> It can hardly be said that the mentally ill patient freely chooses such accommodation. Charging them in these circumstances may be surprising....
> If the argument of the authorities is accepted that there is a power to charge these patients, such a view of the law would not be testimony to our society, attaching a high value to the need to care after the exceptionally vulnerable.

The wariness by the European Court of Human Rights of allowing resource arguments to excuse states from their core 'administration of justice obligations' under Articles 5 and 6[151] has been adopted by our domestic courts; Lord Bingham for instance commenting[152]:

> It is plain that contracting states cannot blame unacceptable delays on a general want of prosecutors or judges or courthouses or on chronic underfunding of the legal system.

R v MHRT and Secretary of State for Health ex parte KB (2002)[153] concerned lengthy delays faced by detained mental health service users, in obtaining a hearing to challenge their detention. Stanley Burnton J noted that although in general "the question whether the Government allocates sufficient resources to any particular area of state activity is not justiciable", this was not the case "when issues are raised under Articles 5 and 6 as to the guarantee of a speedy hearing or of a hearing within a reasonable time". In such situations he held that the onus is on the State to excuse the delay. Applying case law of the Strasbourg Court[154] he considered that delays caused by "a sudden and unpredictable increase in the workload" might be acceptable, but not chronic problems due to "shortages of staff or pressure of work ... or on the lack of suitably trained staff". On analysis he found that the delays in question were attributable to the latter, and accordingly found a violation of Article 5(4).

What emerges from the above review is that a resource argument alone will seldom dispose of a claim to respect for a Convention right. In relation to the absolute Convention Articles, resource arguments will rarely if ever be relevant. In relation to the positive obligations under these Articles (for instance a duty to provide healthcare or social care) the state can play the resource card, but it cannot assume it will trump all others – particularly where the consequences of inaction for the applicant are dire. For some reason, perhaps self-serving, it appears that judges are particularly adverse to the parlous state of government finances being used as an excuse for failing to adequately resource the court and tribunal services.

In relation to the qualified rights, it is likely the extent of available resources will be a relevant factor in determining whether a negative obligation has been respected, although courts will require evidence that the impugned act is 'proportionate' and that the resource difficulties are "made out by evidence, and cannot assumed to be present"[155]. The level of scrutiny will inevitably be less for those positive obligations under the qualified Articles, but again, where the consequences of a failure to act are likely to be severe, then any assertion of poverty by the state will again call for heightened scrutiny by the Court.

In this chapter we have repeatedly noted the relative paucity of complaints to the European Court of Human Rights made by disabled people. Small as the number of applications have been, they do, on analysis, illustrate the important contribution the Court has to make in addressing the severe denial of the fundamental rights of disabled people.

Notes

[1] With the exception of cases concerning mental health detention (under Article 5) where the disabled person will almost invariably have an enforceable right to legal representation.

[2] This proposition may go some way to explain the results of research conducted by the Royal National Institute for the Blind (December 2000) which contrasted the over 5,000 employment tribunal cases that had been brought under the Disability 1995 Discrimination Act with the 25 cases concerning goods and services: Law Society Gazette 97/48, 15 December 2000, p 4.

[3] *Golder v UK* (1975) 1 EHRR 524.

[4] Appointeeship arises when an official of the Department for Work and Pensions decides that a claimant lacks sufficient mental capacity to manage their social security benefits – Regulation 33, 1987 Social Security (Claims and Payments) Regulations.

[5] 22504/93; 17 May 1995.

[6] 22 EHRR CD 148; [1996] EHRLR 526.

[7] 15780/89.

[8] 31534/96; 5 July 1999.

---

[9] Commission Report adopted 20 May 1998, No. 26494/95.

[10] 2 EHRR 305; 9 February 1979.

[11] Sections 1 and 2 of which put advocates ('authorised representatives') on a statutory footing. These Sections have not however been brought into effect because of 'their resource and administrative implications'.

[12] 15780/89.

[13] Four discreet proposals presently exist, namely (1) for NHS patients via Section 12 of the 2001 Health and Social Care Act; (2) for detained mental-health service users, Part 7 of the draft 2002 Mental Health Bill provides for specialist independent mental health advocacy services to be available to everyone who is being treated in accordance with the Bill; (3) for people with learning disabilities as a result of the White Paper 'Valuing People' *Valuing People: A New Strategy for Learning Disability for the 21st Century.* March 2001, Cm 5086 Department of Health and the follow up guidance LAC (2001) 23, para 27; and (4) for disabled children, as a result of the 'Quality Protects' and follow up guidance LAC (2000) 22.

[14] *The Times,* 21December: [2002] HRLR 15; (2002) 5 CCLR 5.

[15] *Hoekstra v HM Advocate (No. 1)* (2000) *The Times,* 14 April: (2000) UKHRR 578: (2000) HRLR 410.

[16] 25290/94; 28 February 1996.

[17] In so deciding it referred to *Stanford v UK* (1994) [23 February 1994; 50/1992/ 395/473], a case where although the defendant had been unable to hear what was being said at his trial (due to the acoustics of a new court) neither he nor his barrister mentioned the problem to the judge. However court procedures/timetables that lead to the exhaustion of parties/lawyers can be 'unfair' under Article 6(1): see for instance *Makhfi v France* 59335/00.

[18] *R v Isleworth Crown Court ex parte King* [2001] ACD 289.

[19] Rule 21.4.3.c, Civil Procedure Rules.

[20] 14 DR 31.

[21] *Pretty v UK* (2002).

[22] EHRR 245 at 305.

[23] *Osman v UK* (1998) 29 EHRR 245 at 278.

[24] [1995] 2 All ER 129, CA.

[25] A special health authority whose role is to "promote clinical and cost-effectiveness by producing clinical guidelines and audits for dissemination throughout the NHS" (Department of Health, 1997, para 7.6).

[26] See for example the complaint in *Cyprus v Turkey* (Commission decision) 28 June 1996; 25781/94, concerning the uneven availability of medical services.

[27] See *R v SS Home Department ex Mahmood* [2001] 1 WLR 840 and *R v SS Home Department, ex parte Daly* (2001) [2001] 2 WLR 1622: [2001] 3 All ER 433.

[28] Very few cases of this nature have reached Strasbourg. Those that have, have concerned allegations of ill-treatment and failure to provide adequate care and have been ruled inadmissible for procedural reasons by the Commission; see *Persson v Sweden* (1993) 3 May 1993 14451/88; *Persson v Sweden* (1996) 21236/93; 25 November 1996 and *Santaniemi v Sweden* (1997) 27594/95; 10 September 1997. See also *Erikson v Italy* (1999) 37900/97; 26 October 1999; *Powell v UK* 45305/99; 4 May 2000 and *Calvelli and Ciglio v Italy* (2002) 32967/96; 17 January 2002.

[29] [1991] Fam 33 [1990] 3 All ER 930, [1990] 2 WLR 140. See also *In re B (a minor: wardship; medical treatment)* [1981] 1 WLR 1421; and *R v Portsmouth Hospitals NHS Trust, ex parte Glass* [1999] 2 FLR 905, 50 BMLR 269.

[30] *In re Superintendent of Family and Child Service and Dawson* (1983) 145 DLR (3d) 610, also reported and referred to *In re C* [1990] Fam 26 as *In re SD* [1983] 3 WWR 618.

[31] This decision was followed in a very similar fact case, *In Re J (a minor: child in care; medical treatment)* [1992] 3 WLR 507: [1992] 4 All ER 614 where the medical view was again that in the case of a life threatening event, intensive therapeutic treatment would be inappropriate. In holding that it could "envisage no circumstances in which it would be right directly or indirectly to require a doctor to treat a patient in a way that was contrary to the doctor's professional judgment" (per Leggatt LJ) particularly when this had an impact on "scarce resources (both human and material) ... without knowing whether or not there are other patients to whom those resources might more advantageously be devoted" (per Balcombe LJ).

[32] [1993] AC 789; [1993] 2 WLR 316; [1993] 1 All ER 821.

[33] *NHS Trust A v Mrs M; NHS Trust B v Mrs H* (2000): (2001) 1 All ER 801: (2001) 2 WLR 942: (2001) 58 BMLR 87.

[34] 65653/01; 21 March 2002.

[35] 34151/96; 1 July 1998.

[36] *See for instance A (a mental patient: sterilisation)* [2000] 1 FLR 549; (2000) 53 BMLR 66 [2000] Fam Law 242 *Re Z (medical treatment: hysterectomy)* (1999) 53 BMLR 53; [2000] 1 FCR 274; [2000] 1 FLR 523; *Re SL (an adult patient: medical treatment)* (2000) CA [2000] 2 FCR 452; (2000) 58 BMLR 105; and in *Re GF (a patient)* (1991) [1991] FCR 786.

[37] [2002] 2 All ER 449: [2002] 65 BMLR 149: [2002] 1 FLR 1090.

[38] 18835/91; 2 December 1992.

[39] *LCB v UK* (1998); 27 EHRR 212.

[40] (1999) 52 BMLR 124, [1999] 2 FCR 577, 29 [1999] Fam Law 753.

[41] *R v Ashworth Hospital Authority ex parte Brady* (2000); 58 BMLR 173.

[42] *Re C (adult: refusal of medical treatment)* ([1994] 1 W.L.R. 290.

[43] 15 EHRR 437.

[44] *R (Wilkinson) v RMO Broadmoor and others*: [2001] EWCA Civ 1545; 5 CCLR 121.

[45] 24 EHRR 423; and see also *Tanko v Finland* (1994) 23634/94; 19 May 1994.

[46] *R v North and East Devon Health Authority ex parte Coughlan* (1999) 2 CCLR 285; [2000] 2 WLR 622: [2000] 51 BMLR 1: [2000] 3 All ER 850 – see below.

[47] *Passannante v Italy* (1998) 32647/96; 1 July 1998, where the Commission held that "an excessive delay of the public health service in providing a medical service to which the patient is entitled and the fact that such delay has, or is likely to have, a serious impact on the patient's health could raise an issue under Article 8(1)". *See also the not unrelated decisions of the European Court of Justice in Geraets-Smits v Stichting: The Times*, 4 September; ECJ 12/7/01 Case C–157/99.

[48] 429 US 97 (1976).

[49] *Soobramoney v Minister of Health (Kwa-Zulu-Natal)* Constitutional Court of South Africa CCT 32/97 (26 November 1997); 50 BMLR 224.

[50] 2 EHRR 305.

[51] What he has, elsewhere referred to as "certain basic rights of individuals should not be capable in any circumstances of being overridden".

[52] *Osman v UK* (1998) 29 EHRR 245.

[53] "the unforeseen catastrophes which could befall any person" per Sachs J in *Soobramoney v Minister of Health (Kwa-Zulu-Natal)* 50 BMLR 224.

[54] per Lord Browne-Wilkinson in *Airedale NHS Trust v Bland* [1993] AC 789; [1993] 2 WLR 316; [1993] 1 All ER 821.

[55] *D v UK* 24 EHRR 423.

[56] *Passannante v Italy* (1998) 32647/96; 1 July 1998.

[57] *Netecki v Poland* (2002) 65653/01; 21 March 2002.

[58] *R v Cambridge Health Authority ex parte B* (1995) [1995] 2 All ER 129, CA.

[59] *R (Wilkinson) v RMO Broadmoor and others*: [2001] EWCA Civ 1545; 5 CCLR 121.

[60] 4 East 103, at 107.

[61] See for example *R (Othman) v SS Work and Pensions* (2001) 5 CCLR 148 at 157; and O'Callaghan and Bhavsar (2001).

[62] *R v Lincolnshire County Council and Wealdon District Council ex parte Atkinson, Wales and Stratford* [1995] Admin LR 529 at p 535.

[63] *R v Hammersmith and Fulham LBC ex parte M, P, A & X* (1996) 1 CCLR 69 at p 83.

[64] *R (Othman) v SS Work and Pensions* (2001) 5 CCLR 148 at pp 158-9.

[65] 1 CCLR 7 at p 16.

[66] 34 EHRR 3.

[67] February 1995 No 231. Part II of the Draft Bill annexed to the Report created a statutory regime by which applications could be made to the Court to obtain protection orders for 'vulnerable adults'.

[68] 100/1997/884/1096; 23 September 1998.

[69] *Re F (an adult: court's jurisdiction)* (2000) 3 CCLR 210; *The Times*, 25 July.

[70] 8978/80; 26 March 1995; 8 EHRR 235.

[71] *The Times*, 13 August; 34 EHRR 1285.

[72] See, for instance, *International Journal of Geriatric Psychiatry*,vol 8, p 521 (1993); also see *The Times* (1994) 7 July, 'Elderly patients die within weeks of transfer'.

[73] 'Relocation of the aged and disabled: A mortality study', *Journal of American Geriatric Society*, vol 11, 185.

[74] 2 CCLR 285 (CA).

[75] See for instance *Assenov v Bulgaria* (1998) 28 EHRR 652; *Labita v Italy* 6/4/2000 and *Santaniemi v Sweden* (1997) 27594/95; 10 September 1997.

[76] 28 EHRR 652.

[77] (1992) 15 EHRR 584.

[78] 2 EHRR 387.

[79] See for instance, *X v UK* 4 EHRR 188; October 24 1981 and *Ashingdane v UK* 7 EHRR 528.

[80] *Ashingdane v UK* (ibid) at paragraph 44. In the case of *Michel Aerts v Belgium* 29 EHRR 50, the Court found a violation of Article 5(1) in relation to the detention of the applicant in the psychiatric wing of a prison which was not an "appropriate establishment" in view of the lack of qualified personnel. The failure to provide medical treatment to a person in detention under Article 5(1)(e) could amount to inhuman treatment contrary to Article 3.

[81] *R v MHRT London South and SW Region ex parte C* (2001) *The Times*, 11 July; [2002] 1 WLR 176.

[82] *R v MHRT, North and East London Region and the Secretary of State for Health, ex parte H* (2001) [2001] 3 WLR 512; [2001] 61 BMLR 163; [2002] QBD 1 *The Times*, 2 April; 4 CCLR 119.

[83] *DN v Switzerland* 27154/95; 29 March 2001.

[84] *Johnson v UK* (1999) 27 EHRR 196.

[85] 26 February 2002.

[86] [1998] 3 WLR 107; [1998] 3 All ER 289.

[87] "less than 10 per cent of mentally disordered patients cared for in hospitals and mental nursing homes are admitted under the provisions of the Mental Health Act 1983" per Lord Steyn in the *Bournewood* judgment.

[88] As amended by the 1951 National Assistance (Amendment) Act which allows for the removal order to be made *ex parte* in cases of urgency.

[89] *Handyside v UK* (1976) 1 EHRR 737.

[90] *Botta v Italy* (1998) 153/1996/772/973, 24 February 1998.

[91] 53176/99; 7 February 2002.

[92] 46544/99; 26 February 2002.

[93] Few Strasbourg complaints have directly addressed the rights of siblings to have contact with each other, but see *Olsson v Sweden (No 1)* (1988) 11 EHRR 259, and *Covezzi and Morselli v Italy*; admissibility decision of 24 January 2002.

[94] *Sutherland v UK* 1 July 1997; 25186/94. [1998] EHRLR 117.

[95] *I v UK* (25680/94) 11 July 2002.

[96] *Durham v Durham* (1885) 10PD 80 and *Park v Park* [1954] P112.

[97] 153/1996/772/973; 24 February 1998; 26 EHRR 241.

[98] *Airey v Ireland* (1979) 2 EHRR 305; 9 February 1979.

[99] *Guerra and Others v Italy* (1998) 26 EHRR 357; 14967/89; 26 February 1998.

[100] 8978/80, 26 March 1995; 8 EHRR 235.

[101] See for instance *Guerra and Others v Italy* (1998) 26 EHRR 357; 14967/89; 26 February 1998; *McGinley and Egan v UK* (1998) 27 EHRR 1; and *LCB v UK* (1998) 27 EHRR 212.

[102] *R v Plymouth CC ex parte S* (2002) 5 CCLR 251, at 265 (CA).

[103] *R v Mid Glamorgan FHSA ex parte Martin* [1995] 1 WLR 110

[104] 25 EHRR 371.

[105] [2000] 1 FLR 909; 26494/95; 20 May 1998.

[106] *R v Plymouth CC ex parte S* (2002) 5 CCLR 251 (CA).

[107] 12 EHRR 36.

[108] *Chapman v UK* (2001) 33 EHRR 399.

[109] 28 EHRR CD 175; 36448/97 4 May 1999.

[110] *Lee v Leeds City Council* (2002) *The Times*, 29 January.

[111] In *O'Rourke v UK* (1999) 26 June 2001 No 39022/97, the Court doubted that occupation of a hotel room for 1 month was sufficient and continuous enough to make it his 'home' for the purposes of Article 8.

[112] 2 CCLR 285.

[113] 527 US 581 (1999).

[114] See in this respect *R v Southwark LBC ex parte Khana and Karim* (2001) (2001) 4 CCLR 267 (CA).

[115] 30548/96; 3 December 1997.

[116] The *Belgian Linguistics Case (No 2)* (1968) 1 EHRR 252.

[117] *McIntyre v UK* (1995) 29046/95; 21 October 1998.

[118] For instance the consolidated cases of *Connolley v UK* 14138/88, *PD v UK* 14137/88 and *P and LD v UK* 14135/88, all decided on 2 October 1989, and *Klerks v Netherlands* 25212/94 4 July 1995.

[119] *See* for example *R v East Sussex County Council ex parte Tandy* [1998] 2 WLR 884: [1998] 2 All ER 769: (1998)1 CCLR 352, where the House of Lords held that resource arguments had little application in relation to local authority special educational needs responsibilities.

[120] 17 EHRR 293.

[121] 26 EHRR 357; 14967/89; 26 February 1998; *McGinley and Egan v UK* (1998) 27 EHRR 1; and *LCB v UK* (1998) 27 EHRR 212.

[122] Citing *Leander v Sweden* (1987) 9 EHRR 433; 26 March 1987.

[123] *Leander v Sweden* (1987) 9 EHRR 433; 26 March 1987.

[124] *Mathieu-Mohin and Clerfaut v Belgium* (1988) 10 EHRR 1; 9267/81; 2 March 1987.

[125] Via Section 4 of the 2000 Representation of the People Act, which makes special provision for patients in mental hospitals who are not detained offenders or on remand, and Section 13, which provides for assistance to disabled people who through 'blindness or other physical incapacity' require the assistance of another person in order to be able to vote.

[126] *McFeeley v UK* (1981) 3 EHRR 161; 8317/78, 15 May 1980.

[127] *Botta v Italy* (1998) 153/1996/772/973, 24 February 1998.

[128] Proposals have been made, via Protocol 12, to amend Article 14 to replace the words "*the rights and freedoms set forth in this Convention*" currently in the Article, with the words "any right set forth by law".

[129] *Anguelova v Bulgaria* 38361/97; 13 June 2002.

[130] In an extreme situation it is possible that very serious and arbitrary discrimination might be considered to be 'degrading treatment' contrary to Article 3. The Commission made such a finding in 1973 in *Patel v UK (the East Africans case)* 3 EHRR 76 in relation to the refusal of British Citizenship to non-white Africans. However the Court has never made such a finding.

[131] 29046/95; 21 October 1998.

[132] That is, comply with the principle of proportionality, discussed above.

[133] 31 EHRR 411.

[134] *The Times*, 13 August: 34 EHRR 1285.

[135] [1995] 2 All ER 129, CA.

[136] The 'Separation of Powers'; Annual Commercial Bar Lecture, (2001) London: unpublished transcript.

[137] *The Times*, 15 March: [2002] 2 WLR 720; [2002] 2 All ER 192.

[138] See for example *Olmstead v L.C.* (1999) 527 US 581 (1999).

[139] See for example the comments of Cooke P in *R v Stack* [1986] 1 NZLR 257.

[140] See for example *Paschim Banga Khet Mazdoor Samity v State of West Bengal* (1996) 4 SCC 37; (1996) 3 SCJ 25.

[141] See for instance *Airey v Ireland* 2 EHRR 305.

[142] *Soobramoney v Minister of Health (Kwa-Zulu-Natal)* Constitutional Court of South Africa CCT 32/97 (26 November 1997); 50 BMLR 224.

[143] 1 CCLR 40; [1997] 2 All ER 1.

[144] In their account of the passage of the Act through parliament, Darnbrough and Kinrade (1995) note "the support of the Treasury was absolutely essential...... In February 1970, the Commons carried a Money Resolution in support of the Bill..."

[145] (1996) 1 CCLR 19 at 38.

[146] (1996) 1 CCLR 40 at 88.

[147] per Lord Lloyd.

[148] Per Lord Browne-Wilkinson in *Airedale NHS Trust v Bland* (1993) [1993] AC 789; [1993] 2 WLR 316; [1993] 1 All ER 821.

[149] 1 CCLR 7 at p 16.

[150] [2002] 3 WLR 584; 4 All ER 124.

[151] See for example, *Zimmermann and Steiner v Switzerland* (1983) 6 EHRR 17.

[152] *Dyer Watson* [2002] SLT 229 the Privy Council at 242.

[153] 2002 WL 498854.

[154] See for instance *Koendjbiharie v Netherlands* (1990) 13 EHRR 820.

[155] Per Mance LJ in *R v Southwark LBC ex parte Khana and Karim* (2001) [2001] 4 CCLR 267.

FIVE

The way forward: policy and practice proposals

Introduction

This final chapter explores some of the ways in which the 1998 Human Rights Act may be made to work for the benefit of disabled children and adults. In any such discussion, it is important to be realistic about the limitations as well as the positive potential of any course of action. The 1998 Human Rights Act has undoubtedly raised expectations and generated considerable excitement. It protects many rights that are of fundamental relevance to disabled people. Nevertheless, it is as well to bear in mind Sir Stephen Sedley's comments prior to the Act coming into force, when he warned that without judicial activism "society's losers and winners will merely become the same losers and winners under a Human Rights Act" (Sedley, 1997, p 458).

Any discussion of the potential impact of the Act on disabled people's human rights, therefore, needs to face four-square, the implications of their relatively powerless position. There is little point in reviewing *solely in principle*, the potential impact of the Act on disabled people's human rights. Any serious debate must also look at the barriers to making it work for them in practice, together with initiatives which might reduce such impediments – without these, access to justice may prove illusory.

It is not appropriate at this stage to be prescriptive about the action which individuals or organisations should take in order to make the Convention rights a concrete reality in the lives of disabled people, since the debate about the range of approaches and their implications is ongoing. It is, however, important to be clear that in recognising the fact that many disabled people are not best placed to gain access to justice, we are not suggesting that they should be characterised as passive, unable to act on situations affecting their lives, or bereft of opinions on matters which impact on their fundamental rights. The chapter explores three main approaches which should clearly not be regarded as mutually exclusive:

- redress for individuals;
- changing the political and public climate;
- changing practice in public authorities.

Redress for individuals

The significance of the 1998 Human Rights Act lies neither in the introduction of any new rights, nor in any ostensible transformation in perceptions as to what is, or is not, good practice. It is important primarily because it provides a new (and at times more precise) language with which to articulate existing concerns about poor or unacceptable practice.

Individuals will continue to seek redress in respect of their grievances through local complaints, the Ombudsman, judicial review and so on, and will additionally be able to express their concerns in terms of their Convention rights if (and it is a big IF) they are aware of these rights. The failure of the government to invest resources in publicising the impact of the Act among the general public has been the subject of criticism (Clements, 1999b) and contrasted with the substantial publicity provided to equivalent legislation in other jurisdictions (Kirby, 1998).

It is important therefore to be realistic about the limitations of individual action. A theme of this text has been the substantial barriers disabled people face in accessing individual remedies. Not only does their social environment frequently undermine their ability to complain, they often experience exhaustion, an ingrained feeling of powerlessness, a general sense of being overwhelmed and a fear of repercussions. In his study of social services complaints procedures, Simons (1995) notes that fear of the consequences was by far the most commonly cited reason for not making formal complaints. It also has to be remembered that people may have to complain about those on whom they depend for essential services.

It takes no feat of imagination to realise how daunting and emotionally disturbing it is for many people to take a complaint or court action against a public body. It also has to be appreciated that the history of 'test case' legal actions is not one of unqualified success: arguably often doing far more to further the conducting lawyer's career than promoting the rights of the alleged victor. In many cases such actions are settled out of court and even when successful, often result in no policy changes by the relevant authority.

Increasing effective access to justice for disabled Individuals

If disabled people are to have a greater opportunity to obtain effective redress, there is no doubt that relevant procedures and practices including those related to litigation, will need to change in order to meet their needs. Already, the provisions of the Disability Discrimination Act require lawyers and courts to make 'reasonable adjustments' to accommodate the needs of disabled people, but (in reality) only after they have actually gained access – or at least plucked up the courage to take this course.

The Human Rights Act also holds out some hope for disabled litigants in respect of the right to a fair trial. Arrangements or practices that can impair access to a fair hearing may be seen to violate their human rights. In recognition of the new environment created by the Act, the Judicial Studies Board (2002) has produced practical guidance for judges, most recently *Equality before the Courts*, a substantial portion of which is devoted to the needs of disabled people. It draws attention to issues raised by disability in the management of a fair trial. It suggests, for example, that particular arrangements may need to be made with regard to a litigant's memory, comprehension and mobility. It argues the need when required, for more frequent breaks for medication, eating and drinking and personal care. It proposes taking into account whether the disabled person can reasonably be kept waiting, when arranging the order in which evidence will be heard. It also recognises that carers or others providing assistance to the disabled person may need to be in close attendance. As we have noted above, the High Court has taken note of earlier guidance and quashed a conviction of a disabled man who had been pressurised to have his case heard when he was exhausted after having to wait over six hours for his case to be called on[1].

The reform of judicial and other forms of procedural remedy (vital though they be) will not however be sufficient to counteract all the difficulties encountered by disabled children and adults. Other measures including different forms of advocacy and representation will be essential.

Disabled people and those close to them have long recognised the importance of advocacy and representation. The potential contribution of advocacy is, as we have discussed above, increasingly being promoted in public policy in relation to 'vulnerable' people. It needs to be acknowledged that this is not an uncontentious issue and approval of any advocacy arrangements is frequently qualified. There has, for example, been long-standing resentment about disabled people having to deal with a range of systems so complex and unresponsive to their needs that their only chance of success is to rely on a specialist of some sort to act as a mediator and interpreter. Thus, Simkins and Tickner (1978), early commentators on the proliferation of impermeable regulations governing essential benefits for disabled people, observed, "... in effect, a new profession has been created – like the high priests of old, to act as intermediary between the layman and the law – in this case the morass of law relating to welfare benefits" (Simkins and Tickner, 1978, p 36), the message here being that advocacy is no substitute for administrative reform.

It is also important to acknowledge the extent to which traditional professional practices have been seen to misrepresent disabled people's interests and take power and control away from them (Morris, 1993; French, 1994; Dunning, 2001). This is not, however, to deny the "long and distinguished history of various kinds of professional advocates working to extend and implement the rights of people with disabilities both through representing individuals as well as lobbying for general changes in the law" (Brandon, 1995, p 15). The fact that some forms of advocacy are 'contested territory' does not however mean that it is not an important vehicle for advancing the interests of disabled people in the present imperfect system.

It is also necessary to recognise that there are a range of approaches to advocacy and representation and that these have a variety of definitions and interpretations (Brandon, 1995). These might include: legal advice and representation, supported individual or group self-advocacy or peer advocacy (Simons, 1992; Brandon, 1995; Goodley, 2000) and citizen or professional advocacy (Brandon, 1995; Dunning, 1995, 2001).

The recognition and support of advocacy arrangements is an important component in any effective response to making the 1998 Human Rights Act work for disabled people. At its heart advocacy involves "people making a case for themselves and advancing their own interests, or representing others and supporting them to secure and exercise their rights on an individual or collective basis" and is "underpinned by the three guiding principles of independence, inclusion and empowerment" (Dunning, 2001, p 7). The subject has however attracted a substantial literature a review of which is beyond the scope of this text (Brandon, 1995; Atkinson, 1999; Dunning, 2001; Henderson and Pochin, 2001).

We have worked from the assumption that seeking the disabled person's wishes, even when these are hard to reach, is central to good practice. It has to be recognised, however, that some people may not have the intellectual capacity to make the required decisions over issues which impact fundamentally on their human rights. They may need someone else to act on their behalf and may be among the most vulnerable to the risk of human rights violations. For such people there is a drastic need for implementation of law reform based upon clearly articulated principles of the type outlined in the Law Commission's proposals, as discussed above (Law Commission, 1995).

So far, we have considered mechanisms which may assist disabled people to gain access to the often daunting and invariably complex legal process. This should not of course obscure the need for reform of the system itself. Two aspects of which could be addressed with relative ease. The first concerns the need to temper the worst aspects of our adversarial system when it puts disabled people at a disadvantage. There is no reason in principle why an inquisitorial approach, of the type familiar in our coroners' courts, tribunals, and complaints procedures, should not be more widely deployed in relevant cases. Such an approach accords the judge greater responsibility for inquiring into the relative merits of the case, and relies less heavily on the physical and emotional endurance and mental capacities of the parties.

The second concerns the need to further widen the remit of the Disability Rights Commission (DRC) and to provide it with a concomitant increase in resources. Although the DRC has power (under the 1999 Disability Rights Commission Act) to conduct formal investigations, serve non-discrimination notices and to support individual cases, it lacks the resources and powers to institute 'popular' actions. Fulfilling this need would enable the DRC to challenge cases, and litigate if necessary, where no 'victim', or group of 'victims' were prepared to come forward and agree to be named parties. In addition, the DRC would be enabled to take test case litigation to clarify the law in certain areas at present outside its remit; for instance the initiation of court proceedings under the HRA (presently outside its powers)[2].

Individual action for redress under the law, important though it may be is largely *reactive* to situations which are unsatisfactory in the first place. Its limitations in other respects have also been debated by disabled people. Oliver challenges the faith that he sees the independent living movement in the US as having placed in individual legal rights. He contrasts this sharply with the approach of the Disabled People's Movement in the UK. He asserts that activists in the UK recognised that the fundamental change in society that was required to bring about full civil rights for disabled people, would only come about as a result of collective action (Oliver, quoted in Campbell and Oliver, 1996, p 204). In the next two sections, therefore, we turn to proactive approaches which may have a more widespread impact on disabled people's human rights.

Changing the political and public climate

A collective approach to promoting disabled people's rights consisting of a whole gamut of related political and intellectual activities has been advocated strongly by activists in the Disabled People's Movement (Campbell and Oliver, 1996). Such an approach can be argued to be an effective means for bringing about change because of the size and nature of the task to be accomplished, because it potentially benefits greater numbers than any individualised approach and also because there is much to be said for being proactive in seizing and setting a new political agenda.

In Chapter 1, we described the ways in which the Disabled People's Movement and different groups within it had changed the face of the public debate on disability over the past two decades. Largely through the efforts of disabled people themselves, disability has been relocated into the arena of human and civil rights. As a consequence, many of the damaging but taken-for-granted elements of disabled people's lives have been challenged as discriminatory and as abuses of civil and human rights.

One of the most impressive aspects of the approach of the Disabled People's Movement and its supporters has been the diversity of contexts in which it has directly or indirectly effected change. Public policy, public services, academic work, the law, the private and voluntary sectors, the arts and the media all reflect a different perspective on disability from that prevalent twenty years ago. While the Disabled People's Movement must be given credit for its influence, there is evidence now of a range of activities by others in the public arena which may also contribute to the raising of awareness and consequently, the potential for extending disabled people's human rights. For example, public policy documents relevant to disabled people, now frequently make their value base explicit and this is often expressed in the language of the social model of disability or human rights (for example, Stevens, 1991; DoH and the Home Office, 2000; DoH, 2001). The Disability Rights Commission itself of course, has set an agenda which targets a wide range of areas in which it wishes to see change for the benefit of disabled people (DRC, 2001).

There are clear indications that disabled academics, activists and organisations representing disabled people's interests are investigating the potential of the Act for making a difference to disabled people's rights (Daw, 2000; DRC, 2001; Morris, 2002). It is to be hoped that others too, will see it as their responsibility to support such efforts. As has been emphasised throughout this text, it is important not only to apply the legislation to issues which have been identified as significant in disabled people's lives but also to explore how the language of human rights found in the new politics of disability translates across to the legal context. If the 1998 Human Rights Act is to have an impact in any great measure on disability rights, it will be crucial for disabled people and those close to them to be made aware by a range of means and in large numbers, of its *practical* significance to important aspects of their lives.

Changing practice in public authorities

The responsibility of public authorities to actively protect human rights is central to the European Convention and the 1998 Human Rights Act: by Article 1 they promise to "secure to everyone within their jurisdiction" its benefits (see Appendix I). This is a particularly crucial responsibility in relation to the needs of disabled people, since public bodies cannot leave it up to individual test cases to move the law forward. How then can public bodies develop their organisational arrangements and practices so as to promote disabled people's rights in accordance with the Act?

In order to understand an approach which public authorities might adopt, one cannot disregard the climate in which they currently operate. Not only are many facing resource constraints, many including those providing social care support to disabled people, also face severe staff shortages due to a workforce recruitment and retention crisis. In addition, they are subject to increasing regulation and audit, the *stated* purpose of which is to drive up standards. While many would concur with the wish to improve standards in all sorts of areas of public service, there is increasing scepticism and cynicism among both staff and outside commentators about the outcomes of such regulatory processes (O'Neill, 2002). Harris (2003, p 94) describes how those being audited, "adapt their behaviour to the audit process, distorting reality so that it conforms to an auditable reality". He outlines the ways in which organisations become engaged in fabricating impression management and performing to the audience of regulation. In short, we can see the dangers of the gap between the substantive practice of those in public organisations and the paper trails that they construct in order to try to pass muster in front of the regulators. It must also be remembered that the construction of 'auditable realities' consumes time and other resources.

In such a climate, it would be surprising if public organisations facing the 1998 Human Rights Act, did not seek help to audit their operations with the

Act in mind. It is probably only a matter of time before someone invents an Human Rights Act Kitemark. Bearing in mind the critiques of current regulation and auditing and the fundamental and philosophical nature of the Convention, any audit is unlikely to be in the interests of the human rights of disabled people. It is one thing for an organisation seriously to review its policy and practice with the essence of the Human Rights Act in mind. It is quite another matter for it to set about a Strasbourg-proofing exercise. The latter may encourage a bunker mentality on human rights which sets out to prove that the organisation conforms to requirements. As a result, while an organisation may appear more human rights-friendly on the surface, this may be largely illusory as far as disabled people are concerned. Further, we would argue that in some cases, the fact that *virtual* human rights safeguards have been put in place, may make an organisation less responsive in reality.

This is not to say that certain principles should not inform an authority's approach to questions that may engage the human rights of disabled people. Such a list would include:

- if there is doubt as to whether your organisation is acting as a 'public authority' (see page 16), then act on the basis that it is;
- lead on principle, not on a technicality;
- reach balanced decisions – and where the issue is not straightforward, apply (and be seen to apply) the proportionality principles (see page 27);
- avoid any form of 'blanket policy' – and what is equally dangerous, 'blanket' thinking;
- justify decisions on the basis of reason – that is, reasonable argument which takes into account individual circumstances, and not solely on the basis of absolutes, custom, policy or indeed 'the law'.
- be prepared to change your approach – in individual cases, or indeed, your established policy where reason dictates;
- above all ensure that the barriers to 'accessing justice' (of the type repeatedly highlighted in this text) are addressed in a concrete and effective way.

It is not, however, at the level of a checklist that implementation of the principles underlying that Act should be approached. If we take health and social care organisations as examples, there are indications that many practitioners wish to practise to genuinely high standards and are demoralised when they perceive that factors beyond their control including resource constraints and additional bureaucracy, get in the way (LGA, 2002). Particularly in the areas of health, education and social care (all crucial to disabled children and adults), much of what is contained in the 1998 Human Rights Act already conforms with what is regarded as best professional and organisational practice. There is now a fairly recent, but nevertheless established, tradition within these fields of promoting equality and challenging practice that is discriminatory or oppressive in relation to disabled children or adults (for example, Reisser and Mason, 1992; Thompson, 1993, 1998; Bywater and McLeod, 1996; Booth, 1999; Oliver and Sapey, 1999; DoH, 2001; Read and Clements, 2001). Many of those practising will have received training which addresses and promotes such dimensions of professional practice and service delivery.

One of the most positive approaches which organisations, managers and practitioners can adopt is to try and see the Human Rights Act as a statutory reinforcer of good practice rather than a hostile and negative addition to the regulatory burden. In an earlier chapter, we referred to the Evans inquiry into the provision and outcome of paediatric cardiac services in two London hospitals (Evans, 2001). The panel's report drew substantially on the Convention and the 1998 Human Rights Act in its efforts both to establish a benchmark against which judgments could be made and to develop model guidance for future best practice. It has to be recognised, however, that for some practitioners and managers, experience of the law and related training has been daunting or inadequate (Read and Clements, 1999). Through staff development programmes, workers may be enabled to explore more positively the implications of the 1998 Human Rights Act in relation to the operations of the organisation and their practice within it. They may also come to realise that for many disabled children and adults, their only opportunity to become aware of, and to extend, their human rights will be through contact with conscientious practitioners whose organisations are seriously attempting to work to the human rights agenda. Practitioners in public organisations may not be best placed to be entirely independent advocates but with the right support, they can in different ways, affirm disabled people's human rights and advocate for them in a proactive way.

It is fitting to close with an example that illustrates many of the elements which we have identified as significant in this book. The case of Peter Chandler was reported in *The Times* on 15 November 1993. He had been disabled as a result of a stroke and was told that he could only attend a local authority day centre provided that he agreed to stay inside an adapted tea-trolley designed to stop him from 'wandering'. The decision was defended by social services managers on the grounds that they could not afford to provide the one-to-one care he required. Mr Chandler described it as "like having a ball and chain around my leg". A lawyer was contacted informally by concerned social workers and as a result of proceedings, Mr Chandler was provided with two volunteers to assist him during the day and ensure his safety and well-being (Laurance, 1993, p 4).

One suspects that no one coming to this situation could have been but appalled by the treatment he received. It can be seen as an example of the way in which essential services may be conjoined with oppression. Mr Chandler felt humiliated, but was powerless. The social workers were uneasy about the situation, but somehow felt unable to do anything to bring about a change of practice within the organisation. Consequently, they resorted to making contact with a lawyer. In the language of the Director of Social Services, the situation was 'regrettable', but there was little that could be done because of resource difficulties. In the language of the Convention, however, it was degrading treatment and contrary to Article 3. Mr Chandler had no power to affect change – he had no access to justice. Action had to come from those conscientious practitioners involved in his care who were witnessing something that was very far removed from anything they knew to be good practice. The practice about which they had misgivings, translated in legal terms as a violation of Mr Chandler's human rights. Further, it could no longer be ignored or justified on the grounds of restricted resources.

Note

[1] *R v Iselworth Crown Court ex parte King* [2001] ACD 289 (see page 45).

[2] See Parliamentary of Lord Ashley of Stoke, HL5742, 15 October 2002; column WA44.

Bibliography

Abberley, P. (1987) 'The concept of oppression and the development of a social theory of disability', *Disability, Handicap and Society*, vol 2, no 11, pp 5-19.

Abberley, P. (1992) 'Counting us out: a discussion of the OPCS disability surveys', *Disability, Handicap and Society*, vol 7, no 2, pp 139-55.

Abberley, P. (1996) 'Work, utopia and impairment', in L. Barton (ed) *Disability and society: Emerging issues and insights*, London: Longman.

Abberley, P. (1997) 'The limits of classical social theory in the analysis and transformation of disablement (can this really be the end; to be stuck inside of Mobile with the Memphis blues again?)', in L. Barton and M. Oliver (eds) *Disability studies: Past, present and future*, Leeds: The Disability Press, pp 25-44.

Abbott, D., Morris, J. and Ward, L. (2000) *Disabled children and residential schools: A survey of local authority policy and practice*, Bristol: Norah Fry Research Centre.

Alzheimer's Society (1998) *Mistreatment of people with dementia and their carers*, London: Alzheimer's Society.

Anderson, H. (1995) *Disabled people and the labour market*, Birmingham: West Midlands Low Pay Unit.

Arai-Takahashi, Y. (2001) 'The role of international health law and the WHO in the regulation of public health', in R. Martin and L. Johnson (eds) *Law and the public dimension of health*, London: Cavendish, pp 143-72.

Arnold, P. (1993) *Community care: The housing dimension*, York: Joseph Rowntree Foundation.

Atkinson, D. (1999) *Advocacy: A review*, Brighton: Pavillion Publishing for the Joseph Rowntree Foundation.

Audit Commission (1996) *Balancing the care equation*, London: The Stationery Office.

Audit Commission (1998) *Home alone: The role of housing in community care*, London: Audit Commission Publications.

Baldwin, S. (1985) *The costs of caring: Families with disabled children*, London: Routledge and Kegan Paul.

Baldwin, S. and Carlisle, J. (1994) *Social support for disabled children and their families: A review of the literature*, Edinburgh: HMSO.

Ball, M. (1998) *Disabled children: Directions for their future care*, London: DoH (in association with the SSI and the Council for Disabled Children).

Barnardo's Policy Development Unit (1996) *Transition into adulthood*, Barkingside: Barnardo's.

Barnes, C. (1991) *Disabled people in Britain and discrimination*, London: Hurst & Company in Association with the British Council of Organisations of Disabled People.

Barnes, H., Thornton, P. and Maynard Campbell, S. (1998) *Disabled people and employment: A review of research and development work*, Bristol: The Policy Press.

Barton, L. (1986) 'The politics of special educational needs', *Disability, Handicap and Society*, vol 1, no 3, pp 273-90.

Barton, L. (1996) (ed) *Disability and society: Emerging issues and insights*, London: Longman.

BBC (1998) 'Here and now', Manchester, 1 June 1998.

Beecher, W. (1998) *Having a say! Disabled children and effective partnership in decision making. Section II: Practice initiatives and selected annotated references*, London: Council For Disabled Children.

Beresford, B. (1995) *Expert opinions: A national survey of parents caring for a severely disabled child*, Bristol/York: The Policy Press/Joseph Rowntree Foundation.

Beresford, B., Sloper, P., Baldwin, S. and Newman, T. (1996) *What works in services for families with a disabled child*, Barkingside: Barnardo's.

Bertoud, R., Lakey, J. and McKay, S. (1993) *The economic problems of disabled people*, London: Policy Studies Institute.

Beveridge, W.M. (1942) *Social insurance and allied services*, Cmd 6404, London: HMSO.

Billis, D. and Harris, M. (eds) (1996) *Voluntary agencies: Challenges of organisation and management*, Basingstoke: Macmillan.

Birch, D. (2000) 'A better deal for vulnerable witnesses?', *Criminal Law Review*, April, pp 223-49.

Bond, N. (1971) 'The case for radical casework', *Social Work Today*, vol 2, no 9, pp 11-12.

Booth, T. (1992) *Reading critically*, Unit 10, E241, Milton Keynes: Open University.

Booth, T. (1999) 'Inclusion and exclusion policy in England: who controls the agenda?', in F. Armstrong, D. Armstrong and L. Barton (eds) *Inclusive education: Policy, contexts and comparative perspectives*, London: Fulton, pp 14-28.

Booth, T. and Booth, W. (1994) *Parenting under pressure. Mothers and fathers with learning difficulties*, Buckingham: Open University Press.

Booth, T., Simons, K. and Booth, W. (1990) *Outward bound: Relocation and community care for people with learning difficulties*, Buckingham: Open University Press.

Booth, T., Swann, W., Masterson, M. and Potts, P. (eds) (1992) *Curricula for diversity in education*, London: Routledge in association with the Open University.

Brandon, D. with Brandon, A. and Brandon, T. (1995) *Advocacy power to people with disabilities*, Birmingham: Venture Press.

Brown, H. and Craft, A. (eds) (1989) *Thinking the unthinkable: Papers on sexual abuse and people with learning difficulties*, London: FPA Education Unit.

Bynoe, I., Oliver, M. and Barnes, C. (1991) *Equal rights for disabled people*, London: Institute for Public Policy Research.

Bywaters, P. and McLeod, E. (eds) (1996) *Working for equality in health*, London: Routledge.

Campbell, J. and Oliver, M. (1996) *Disability politics*, London: Routledge.

Cavet, J. (1998) 'Leisure and friendship', in C. Robinson and K. Stalker (eds) *Growing up with disability*, London: Jessica Kingsley Publishers, pp 97-110.

CCETSW (Central Council for Education and Training in Social Work) (1987) *Policy, politics and practice training for work with mentally handicapped people*, Rugby: CCETSW.

Clements, L. (1999a) 'Weighting for justice: the 1998 Human Rights Act and mental health care law', *Mental Health Care Journal*, vol 2, no 7, pp 224-5, March.

Clements, L. (1999b) 'The 1998 Human Rights Act – a new equity of a new opiate: reinventing justice or repackaging state control?', *Journal of Law and Society*, vol 26, no 1, March, pp 72-85.

Clements, L. (2000) *Community care and the law*, London: Legal Action Group.

Clements, L. (2002) 'Community care law and the 1998 Human Rights Act', in B. Bytheway, V. Bacigalupo, J. Bornat, J. Johnson and S. Spurr (eds) *Understanding care, welfare and community: A reader*, London: Routledge, pp 247-54.

Clements, L., Mole, N. and Simmons, A. (1999) *European human rights: Taking a case under the Convention* (2nd edn), London: Sweet & Maxwell.

Clements, L., Thomas, P. and Thomas, R. (1997) 'The rights of minorities', in *OSCE* Bulletin (Warsaw), vol 4, no 4, Fall 1996, pp 3-10.

Cochrane, A. (1993) *Whatever happened to local government?*, Buckingham: Open University Press.

Cross, M. (1992) 'Abusive practices and disempowerment of children with physical impairments', *Child Abuse Review*, vol 1, no 3, pp 194-7.

Crow, L. (1996) 'Including all of our lives', in J. Morris (ed) *Encounters with strangers: Feminism and disability*, London: The Women's Press, pp 206-26.

Dalrymple, J. and Burke, B. (1995) *Anti-oppressive practice: Social care and the law*, Buckingham: Open University Press.

Darnbrough, A. and Kinrade, D. (1995) *Be it enacted*, London: RADAR.

Daw, R. (2000) *The impact of the 1998 Human Rights Act on disabled people*, A report prepared for the Disability Rights Commission and the Royal National Institute for Deaf People, London: RNID.

Dawson, J. (1999) 'Necessitous detention and the informal patient', *Legal Quarterly Review*, no 115, pp 40-6, April.

DfE (Department for Education) (1994) *Code of practice on the identification and assessment of special needs in education*, London: DfE.

DfEE (Department for Education and Employment) (1998) *Excellence for all children, meeting special educational needs*, London: The Stationery Office.

DES (Department of Education and Science) (1978) *The Report of the Committee of Enquiry into the Education of Handicapped Children and Young People* (Warnock Report), Cmnd 7212, London: HMSO.

DoH (Department of Health) (1995) *Child protection: Messages from research*, London: HMSO.

DoH (1997) *The new NHS: Modern, dependable*, Cm 3807, London: The Stationery Office.

DoH (1998) *Modernising social services*, Cm 4169, London: The Stationery Office.

DoH (2000) *Assessing children in need and their families: Practice guidance*, London: The Stationery Office.

DoH (2001) *Valuing people: A new strategy for learning disability for the 21st century*, Cm 5086, London: The Stationery Office.

DoH (2002a) 'Draft Mental Health Bill', Cm 5538-I, London: DoH.

DoH (2002b) 'Explanatory Memorandum to the Draft Mental Health Bill 2002', Cm 5538-II, London: DoH.

DHSS (Department of Health and Social Security) (1969) *Report of the Committee of Enquiry into allegations of ill-treatment and other irregularities at Ely Hospital, Cardiff* (Howe Report), Cmnd 3785, London: HMSO.

DHSS (1971) *Better services for the mentally handicapped*, Cmnd 4683, London: HMSO.

DoH and the Home Office (2000) *No secrets: Guidance on developing and implementing multi-agency policies and procedures to protect vulnerable adults from abuse*, London: DoH.

Dickenson, D. and Shah, A. (1999) 'The Bournewood judgment: a way forward?', *Medical Science Law*, vol 39, no 4, pp 280-4.

DRC (Disability Rights Commission) (2001) *Annual Review 2000-2001*, London: DRC.

Dobson, B. and Middleton, S. (1998) *Paying to care: The cost of childhood disability*, York: York Publishing Services for the Joseph Rowntree Foundation.

Doyle, B. (1997) 'Enabling legislation or dissembling law? The 1995 Disability Discrimination Act', *Modern Law Review*, vol 60, no 1, 64-78, January.

Drake, R. (1999) *Understanding disability policies*, Basingstoke: Macmillan Press.

Dunning, A. (1995) *Citizen advocacy with older people: A code of good practice*, London: Centre for Policy on Ageing.

Dunning, A. with Avila, B., Duncan, M. and Miles, J. of the Older People's Advocacy Alliance (OPAAL) UK (2001) *Dignity on the ward: Advocacy with older people in hospital*, London: Help the Aged.

Enticott, J., Graham, P. and Lamb, B. (1992) *Polls apart: Disabled people and the 1992 General Election*, London: Scope.

Evans Report (2001a) *The report of the independent inquiries into paediatric cardiac services at the Royal Brompton Hospital and Harefield Hospital*, London: Royal Brompton Hospital.

Evans Report (2001b) *The summary report of the independent inquiries into paediatric cardiac services at the Royal Brompton Hospital and Harefield Hospital*, London: Royal Brompton Hospital.

Fairbairn, G. (1988) 'Kuhse, Singer and slippery slopes', *Journal of Medical Ethics*, vol 14, no 3, pp 132-4.

Fennell, P. (1999) 'The third way in mental health policy: negative rights, positive rights, and the convention', in L. Clements and J. Young (eds) *Human rights: Changing the culture*, Oxford: Blackwell Publishers, pp 103-27.

Finkelstein, V. (1980) *Attitudes and disabled people: Issues for discussion*, New York, NY: World Rehabilitation Fund.

Fitzgerald, J. (1998) *Time for freedom?*, London: Centre for Policy on Ageing/ Values into Action.

Flynn, L. (1999) 'The implications of Article 13 EC – after Amsterdam, will some forms of discrimination be more equal than others?', *Common Market Law Review*, vol 36, no 6, pp 11-27.

Fordham, M. and de la Mare, T. (2001) 'Identifying the principles of proportionality', in J. Jowell and J. Cooper (eds) *Understanding human rights principles*, Oxford: Hart Publishing, pp 27-87.

French, S. (1996) 'Out of sight, out of mind: the experience and effects of a "special residential school"', in J. Morris (ed) *Encounters with strangers: Feminism and disability*, London: The Women's Press, pp 17-47.

French, S. (1994b) 'Disabled people and professional practice', in S. French (ed) *On equal terms*, London: Butterworth and Heinemann, pp 103-18.

Genugten, W.V. and Perez-Bustillo, C. (eds) (2001) *The poverty of rights*, London: Zed Books.

Glover, N. (1999) 'Capacity to consent – informal admission – mental health – treatment', *Journal of Social Welfare and Family Law*, vol 21, no 2, pp 151-7.

Goodley, D. (2000) *Self advocacy in the lives of people with learning difficulties*, Buckingham: Open University Press.

Gordon, D., Parker, R. and Loughran, F. with Heslop, P. (2000) *Disabled children in Britain. A re-analysis of the OPCS Disability Surveys*, London: The Stationery Office.

Gostin, L. and Mann, J. (1999) 'Towards the development of a human rights impact assessment for the formulation and evaluation of public health policies', in J.M. Mann, S. Gruskin, M.A. Grodin and G.J. Annas (eds) *Health and human rights*, London: Routledge, pp 54-72.

Gray, M. (1979) 'Forcing old people to leave their homes', *Community Care*, 8 March, p 12.

Harker, M. and King, N. (1999) *An ordinary home: Housing and support for people with learning disabilities*, London: IDeA.

Harris, A.I. (1971) *Handicapped and impaired in Great Britain*, London: OPCS, HMSO.

Harris, J. (2003) *The social work business*, London: Routledge.

Harris, J.W. (2002) 'Rights and resources: libertarians and the right to life', *Ratio Juris*, vol 15, no 2, June, pp 109-21.

Hasler, F., Campbell, J. and Zarb, G. (1999) *Direct routes to independence: A guide to local authority implementation and management of direct payments*, London: National Council for Independent Living/Policy Studies Institute.

Henderson, R. and Pochin, M. (2001) *A right result? Advocacy, justice and empowerment*, Bristol: The Policy Press.

Hendriks, A. (1999) 'Disabled persons and their right to equal treatment', in J.M. Mann, S. Gruskin, M.A. Grodin and G.J. Annas (eds) *Health and human rights*, London: Routledge, pp 113-29.

Herberg, J., Le Sueur, A. and Mulcahy, J. (2001) 'Determining civil rights and obligations', in J. Jowell and J. Cooper, *Understanding human rights principles*, Oxford: Hart Publishing, pp 91-138.

Hirst, M. and Baldwin, S. (1994) *Unequal opportunities*, London: HMSO.

Hoffman, L. (1999) 'Human rights and the House of Lords', *Modern Law Review*, no 62, p 159.

Hoffman, L. (2001) 'The separation of powers', Annual Commercial Bar Lecture, unpublished transcript, London: COMBAR.

Holliday, I. (1992) *The NHS transformed*, Manchester: Baseline Books.

Holzhausen, E. and Perlman, V. (2000) *Caring on the breadline: The financial implications of caring*, London: Carers National Association.

Home Office (2000) *Setting the boundaries: Reforming the law on sex offences*, London: Home Office.

Howard, H. (1998) 'Seventy thousand mentally incapacitated denied protection', *Solicitors' Journal*, vol 142, no 27, pp 642-3.

Humphries, S. and Gordon, P. (1992) *Out of sight: The experience of disability 1900-1950*, Plymouth: Northcote House Publishers.

Johnson, P. (1981) 'Selective non-treatment and spina bifida: a case study in ethical theory and application', *Bioethics Quarterly*, vol 3, no 2, pp 91-111.

Jones, R. (1999) *Mental Health Act Manual London* (6th edn), London: Sweet & Maxwell.

Judicial Studies Board (2002) *Equality before the courts: A short practical guide for judges*, London: Judicial Studies Board.

Kennedy, M. (1992) 'Not the only way to communicate: a challenge to the voice in child protection work', *Child Abuse Review*, vol 1, no 3, pp 169-77.

Kestenbaum, A. (1998) *Work, rest and play: The deal for personal assistance users*, York: York Publishing Services.

Kirby, M. (1998) 'Freedom of information: the seven deadly sins', *European Human Rights Law Review*, Issue 3, p 245.

Knight, A. (1998) *Valued or forgotten? Independent visitors and disabled young people*, London: National Children's Bureau.

Kuhse, H. (1984) 'A modern myth – that letting die is not the intentional causation of death: some reflections on the trial and acquittal of Dr Leonard Arthur', *Journal of Applied Philosophy*, vol 1, no 1, pp 21-38.

Laurance, J. (1993) 'Stroke victim was kept in tea trolley', *The Times*, 15 November.

Law Commission (1995) *Mental incapacity*, Law Commission Paper No 231, London: HMSO.

Law Commission (2000) 'Consent in sex offences: a policy paper', in Home Office (2000) *Setting the boundaries: Reforming the law on sex offences* (as Appendix C), London: Home Office, pp 9-45.

Lawton, D. (1998) *Complex numbers: Families with more than one disabled child*, York: Social Policy Research Unit, University of York.

LGA (Local Government Association) (2002) *Care to stay? A report into the recruitment and retention of social work and social care staff*, London: LGA.

Lonsdale, S. (1990) *Women and disability*, Basingstoke: Macmillan.

Lord Chancellor's Department (1997) *Who decides?*, Cm 3803, London: The Stationery Office.

Lord Chancellor's Department (1999) *Making decisions*, Cm 4465, London: The Stationery Office.

Loughran, F., Parker, R. and Gordon, D. (1992) *Children with disabilities in communal establishments: A further analysis of the Office of Population Censuses and Surveys Investigation*, Bristol: University of Bristol.

Low, C. (1996) 'Disability models or muddles?', *Therapy Weekly*, February, pp 5-6.

Mahendra, B. (1998) 'No consent, no treatment', *New Law Journal*, vol 148, pp 682-8.

Mann, J.M., Gruskin, S., Grodin, M.A. and Annas, G.J. (eds) (1999) *Health and human rights*, London: Routledge.

Marchant, R. and Page, M. (1992) 'Bridging the gap: investigating the abuse of children with multiple disabilities', *Child Abuse Review 1*, pp 179-83.

Mathew, D., Brown, P., McCreadie, C. and Askham, J. (2002) 'The response to no secrets', *The Journal of Adult Protection*, vol 4, no 1, pp 14-21.

McCarthy, M. (ed) (1989) *The new politics of welfare: An agenda for the 1990s?*, Basingstoke: Macmillan.

Morris, J. (1991) *Pride against prejudice: Transforming attitudes to disability*, London: The Women's Press.

Morris, J. (1993) *Independent lives: Community care and disabled people*, Basingstoke: Macmillan.

Morris, J. (1995) *Gone missing? A research and policy review of disabled children living away from home*, London: Who Cares Trust.

Morris, J. (1997) *Community care: Working in partnership with service users*, Birmingham: Venture Press.

Morris, J. (1998a) *Still missing? vol 1: The experiences of disabled children living away from their families*, London: Who Cares Trust.

Morris, J. (1998b) *Still missing? vol 2: Disabled children and the Children Act*, London: Who Cares Trust.

Morris, J. (1998c) *Accessing human rights: Disabled children and the Children Act*, Barkingside: Barnardo's.

Morris, J. (1999a) *Move on up: Supporting disabled children in the transition to adulthood*, Barkingside: Barnardo's.

Morris, J. (1999b) *Hurtling into the void: Transition to adulthood for young disabled people with 'complex health and support needs'*, Brighton: Pavillion Publishing.

Morris, J. (2002) *A lot to say! A guide for social workers, personal advisors and others working with disabled children and young people with communication impairments*, London: Scope.

Morris, J. and Keith, L. (1995) 'Easy targets: a disability rights perspective on the 'children as carers debate', in J. Morris (ed) *Encounters with strangers: Feminism and disability*, London: The Women's Press.

National Assembly for Wales (2000) *In safe hands*, Cardiff: National Assembly for Wales.

Nozick, R. (1974) *Anarchy, state and utopia*, Oxford: Blackwell.

O'Callaghan, D. and Bhavsar, R. (2001) 'Judicial review and the law of humanity', *Judicial Review*, vol 25.

Oldman, C. and Beresford, B. (1998) *Homes unfit for children: Housing, disabled children and their families*, Bristol/York: The Policy Press/Joseph Rowntree Foundation.

Oliver, M. (1983) *Social work with disabled people*, London and Basingstoke: Macmillan.

Oliver, M. (1990) *The politics of disablement*, London: Macmillan.

Oliver, M. (1996) *Understanding disability*, London: Macmillan.

Oliver, M. and Sapey, B. (1999) *Social work with disabled people* (2nd edn), Basingstoke: Macmillan.

O'Neill, O. (2002) *A question of trust: The BBC Reith Lectures 2002*, Cambridge: Cambridge University Press.

OPCS (Office of the Population Censuses and Surveys) (1989) *Surveys of disability in Great Britain*, Reports 1-6, London: HMSO.

Oswin, M. (1971) *The empty hours*, London: Allen Lane, the Penguin Press.

Oswin, M. (1978) *Children living in long-stay hospitals*, London: Spastics International/Heinemann.

Oswin, M. (1998) 'An historical perspective', in C. Robinson and K. Stalker (eds) *Growing up with disability*, London: Jessica Kingsley Publishers, pp 29-41.

Parker, C. (1996) 'The right to vote', *New Law Journal*, Sept 13, p 132.

Quinn, G. and Degener, T. (2002) *Human rights and disability*, Geneva: UN.

Rafael, D. (1988) 'Handicapped infants: medical ethics and the law', *Journal of Medical Ethics*, vol 14, no 1, pp 5-10.

Read, J. (1987a) 'The structural position of mentally handicapped adults, children and their families: implications for practice', in CCETSW *Policy, politics and practice training for work with mentally handicapped people*, Rugby: CCETSW, pp 14-25.

Read, J. (1987b) 'A problem in the family: explanations under strain', in T. Booth and D. Coulby (eds) *Producing and reducing disaffection: Curricula for all*, Milton Keynes: Open University Press, pp 189-206.

Read, J. (1998) 'Conductive education and the politics of disablement', *Disability and Society*, vol 13, no 2, pp 279-3.

Read, J. (2000) *Disability, the family and society: Listening to mothers*, Buckingham: Open University Press.

Read, J. and Clements, L. (1999) 'Disabled children and the law: an approach to staff development in a local authority', *Local Governance*, vol 25, no 2, pp 87-95.

Read, J. and Clements, L. (2001) *Disabled children and the law: Research and good Practice*, London: Jessica Kingsley Publishers.

Read, J. and Harrison, C. (2002) 'Disabled children living away from home in the UK: recognising hazards and promoting good practice', *Journal of Social Work*, vol 2, no 2, pp 211-31.

Reisser, R. and Mason, M. (1992) *Disability, equality in the classroom: A human rights Issue*, London: Disability Equality in Education.

Robson, P. and Kjønstad, A. (eds) (2001) *Poverty and the law*, Oxford: Hart Publishing.

Royal Commission on Long-Term Care (1999) *With respect to old age*, Cm 4192-I, London: The Stationery Office.

Russell, P. (1998) *Having a say! Disabled children and effective partnership in decision making. Section I: The Report*, London: Council for Disabled Children.

Russell, P. (1995) *Positive choices: Services for disabled children living away from home*, London: Council for Disabled Children.

Ryan, J. and Thomas, F. (1980) *The politics of mental handicap*, Harmondsworth: Penguin.

Sanders, A. (1997) *Victims with learning disabilities: Negotiating the criminal justice system*, Oxford: Oxford University Press.

Scott, R. and Morris, G. (2001) *Polls apart 3*, London: Scope.

Sedley, S. (1997) 'First steps towards a Constitutional Bill of Rights', *European Human Rights Law Review*, Issue 5, pp 458-65.

Seebohm Committee (1968) *Report of the committee on local authority and allied personal social services*, Cmnd 3703, London: HMSO.

Shakespeare, T. (1994) 'Cultural representations of disabled people: dustbins for disavowel', *Disability and Society*, vol 9, no 3, pp 283-301.

Shakespeare, T., Gillespie-Sells, K. and Davies, D. (1996) *The sexual politics of disability*, London: Cassell.

Shaw, L. (1998) 'Children's exeriences of school', in C. Robinson and K. Stalker (eds) *Growing up with disability*, London: Jessica Kingsley Publishers, pp 73-84.

Shearer, A. (1981) *Disability: Whose handicap?*, Oxford: Basil Blackwell.

Shearer, A. (1982) *Living independently*, London: King's Fund.

Shearer, A. (1984) *Everybody's ethics*, London: The Campaign for Mentally Handicapped People.

Simkins, J. and Tickner, V. (1978) *Whose benefit? Uncertainties of cash benefits for the handicapped*, London: Economist Intelligence Unit.

Simons, K. (1992) *Sticking up for yourself: Self-advocacy and people with learning difficulties*, York: Joseph Rowntree Foundation.

Simons, K. (1995) *I'm not complaining, but ...*, York: Joseph Rowntree Foundation.

Simons, K. (1998) *Home, work and exclusion: The social policy implications of supported living and employment for people with learning disabilities*, York: York Publishing Services.

Sinason, V. (1992) *Mental handicap and the human condition: New approaches from the Tavistock*, Free Association Press, pp 281-2.

Slope, P., Knussen, C., Turner, S. and Cunningham, C. (1990) 'Social life of school children with Down's syndrome', *Child: Care, Health and Development*, no 16, pp 235-51.

Smith, A. (1994) 'Damaging experience: black disabled children and educational and social services provision', in N. Begum, M. Hill and A. Stevens (eds) *Reflections: The views of black disabled people on their lives and community care*, London: CCETSW, pp 46-58.

Smith, A. (1998) *"I'm used to it now..." Disabled women in residential care*, London: Greater London Association of Disabled People.

Spastics Society (1992) *A hard act to follow*, London: The Spastics Society.

Starmer, K. (1999) *European human rights law*, London: Legal Action Group.

Stevens, A. (1991) *Disability issues: Developing anti-discriminatory practice*, London: CCETSW.

Stevenson, O. (ed) (1989) *Child abuse: Professional practice and public policy*, Hemel Hempstead: Harvester Wheatsheaf.

Sutherland, A. (ed) (1981) *Disabled we stand*, London: Souvenir Press.

Sutton, A. (1982) *The powers that be*, Unit 8, Course E241 Special Needs in Education, Milton Keynes: The Open University.

Teather, D. (2002) 'Lesbian couple have deaf baby by choice', *The Guardian*, 8 April.

Thomas, D. (1982) *The experience of handicap*, London: Methuen.

Thompson, N. (1998) *Promoting equality: Challenging discrimination and oppression in the human services*, Basingstoke: Palgrave.

Thompson, N. (1993) *Anti-discriminatory practice*, Basingstoke: Palgrave.

Thorold, O. (1996) 'The implications of the European Convention on Human Rights for UK mental health legislation', *European Human Rights Law Review*, vol 6, p 619.

Topliss, E. (1975) *Provision for the disabled*, Oxford and London: Basil Blackwell and Martin Robertson.

Tyne, A. (1982) 'Community care and mentally handicapped people', in A. Walker (ed) *Community care: The family, the state and social policy*, Oxford: Basil Blackwell and Martin Robertson, pp 141-58.

UPIAS (Union of the Physically Impaired Against Segregation) (1976) *The fundamental principles of disability*, London: UPIAS

Walker, A. (1980) 'The social origins of impairment, disability and handicap', *Medicine and Society*, vol 6, no 2, pp 18-26.

Walker. A. (1982) *Unqualified and underemployed: Handicapped young people in the labour market*, London: Macmillan.

Ward, L. (1990) 'A programme for change: current issues in services for people with learning difficulties', in T. Booth (ed) *Better lives: Changing services for people with learning difficulties*, London: *Community Care*/Joint Unit for Social Services Research, pp 1-17.

Wates, M. (2001) *Supporting disabled parents in their parenting role*, York: York Publishing Services for the Joseph Rowntree Foundation.

Westcott, H. (1993) *Abuse of children and adults with disabilities*, London: NSPCC.

Westcott, H. (1998) 'Disabled children and child protection', in C. Robinson and K. Stalker (eds) *Growing up with disability*, London: Jessica Kingsley Publishers, pp 129-42.

Wexler, S. (1970) 'Practicing law for poor people', *Yale Law Journal*, vol 79, pp 1049-50.

Whittle, R. (2000) 'Disability rights after Amsterdam, the way forward', *European Human Rights Law Review 2000*, vol 1, p 33.

Williams, G. (1996) 'Representing disabilities: some questions of phenomenology and politics', in C. Barnes and G. Mercer (eds) *Exploring the divide: Illness and disability*, Leeds: The Disability Press, pp 194-212.

Winterson, J. (2002) 'How would we feel if blind women claimed the right to a blind baby?', London: *The Guardian*, 9 April.

Witting, C. (2001) 'National Health Service rationing: implications for the standard of care in negligence', *Oxford Journal of Legal Studies*, vol 21, no 3, pp 443-71.

Wolfensberger, W. (1980) 'A call to wake up to the beginning of a new wave of "euthenasia" of severely impaired people', *Education Training and Mental Retardation*, vol 15, no 3, pp 171-2.

Younghusband, E., Birchall, D., Davie, R. and Kellmer Pringle, M.L. (1970) *Living with handicap*, London: National Children's Bureau.

Zarb, G. (1995) *Removing disabling barriers*, London: Policy Studies Institute.

The substantive Articles
of the Convention

Article 1

Obligation to respect human rights
The High Contracting Parties shall secure to everyone within their jurisdiction the rights and freedoms defined in Section I of this Convention.

Article 2

Right to life
1. Everyone's right to life shall be protected by law. No one shall be deprived of his life intentionally save in the execution of a sentence of a court following his conviction of a crime for which this penalty is provided by law.
2. Deprivation of life shall not be regarded as inflicted in contravention of this Article when it results from the use of force which is no more than absolutely necessary:
    (a) in defence of any person from unlawful violence;
    (b) in order to effect a lawful arrest or to prevent the escape of a person lawfully detained;
    (c) in action lawfully taken for the purpose of quelling a riot or insurrection.

Article 3

Prohibition of torture
No one shall be subjected to torture or to inhuman or degrading treatment or punishment.

Article 4

Prohibition of slavery and forced labour
1. No one shall be held in slavery or servitude.
2. No one shall be required to perform forced or compulsory labour.
3. For the purpose of this Article the term 'forced or compulsory labour' shall not include:

(a) any work required to be done in the ordinary course of detention imposed according to the provisions of Article 5 of this Convention or during conditional release from such detention;

(b) any service of a military character or, in the case of conscientious objectors in countries where they are recognised, service exacted instead of compulsory military service;

(c) any service exacted in case of an emergency or calamity threatening the life or well-being of the community;

(d) any work or service which forms part of normal civic obligations.

Article 5

Right to liberty and security

1. Everyone has the right to liberty and security of person. No one shall be deprived of his liberty save in the following cases and in accordance with a procedure prescribed by law:

(a) the lawful detention of a person after conviction by a competent court;

(b) the lawful arrest or detention of a person for non-compliance with the lawful order of a court or in order to secure the fulfilment of any obligation prescribed by law;

(c) the lawful arrest or detention of a person effected for the purpose of bringing him before the competent legal authority on reasonable suspicion of having committed an offence or when it is reasonably considered necessary to prevent his committing an offence or fleeing after having done so;

(d) the detention of a minor by lawful order for the purpose of educational supervision or his lawful detention for the purpose of bringing him before the competent legal authority;

(e) the lawful detention of persons for the prevention of the spreading of infectious diseases, of persons of unsound mind, alcoholics or drug addicts or vagrants;

(f) the lawful arrest or detention of a person to prevent his effecting an unauthorised entry into the country or of a person against whom action is being taken with a view to deportation or extradition.

2. Everyone who is arrested shall be informed promptly, in a language which he understands, of the reasons for his arrest and of any charge against him.

3. Everyone arrested or detained in accordance with the provisions of paragraph 1(c) of this Article shall be brought promptly before a judge or other officer authorised by law to exercise judicial power and shall be entitled to trial within a reasonable time or to release pending trial. Release may be conditioned by guarantees to appear for trial.

4. Everyone who is deprived of his liberty by arrest or detention shall be entitled to take proceedings by which the lawfulness of his detention shall be decided speedily by a court and his release ordered if the detention is not lawful.

5. Everyone who has been the victim of arrest or detention in contravention of the provisions of this Article shall have an enforceable right to compensation.

Article 6

Right to a fair trial

1. In the determination of his civil rights and obligations or of any criminal charge against him, everyone is entitled to a fair and public hearing within a reasonable time by an independent and impartial tribunal established by law. Judgment shall be pronounced publicly but the press and public may be excluded from all or part of the trial in the interest of morals, public order or national security in a democratic society, where the interests of juveniles or the protection of the private life of the parties so require, or to the extent strictly necessary in the opinion of the court in special circumstances where publicity would prejudice the interests of justice.
2. Everyone charged with a criminal offence shall be presumed innocent until proved guilty according to law.
3. Everyone charged with a criminal offence has the following minimum rights
   (a) to be informed promptly, in a language which he understands and in detail, of the nature and cause of the accusation against him;
   (b) to have adequate time and facilities for the preparation of his defence;
   (c) to defend himself in person or through legal assistance of his own choosing or, if he has not sufficient means to pay for legal assistance, to be given it free when the interests of justice so require;
   (d) to examine or have examined witnesses against him and to obtain the attendance and examination of witnesses on his behalf under the same conditions as witnesses against him;
   (e) to have the free assistance of an interpreter if he cannot understand or speak the language used in court.

Article 7

No punishment without law

1. No one shall be held guilty of any criminal offence on account of any act or omission which did not constitute a criminal offence under national or international law at the time when it was committed. Nor shall a heavier penalty be imposed than the one that was applicable at the time the criminal offence was committed.
2. This Article shall not prejudice the trial and punishment of any person for any act or omission which, at the time when it was committed, was criminal according to the general principles of law recognised by civilised nations.

Article 8

Right to respect for private and family life
1. Everyone has the right to respect for his private and family life, his home and his correspondence.
2. There shall be no interference by a public authority with the exercise of this right except such as is in accordance with the law and is necessary in a democratic society in the interests of national security, public safety or the economic well-being of the country, for the prevention of disorder or crime, for the protection of health or morals, or for the protection of the rights and freedoms of others.

Article 9

Freedom of thought, conscience and religion
1. Everyone has the right to freedom of thought, conscience and religion; this right includes freedom to change his religion or belief and freedom, either alone or in community with others and in public or private, to manifest his religion or belief, in worship, teaching, practice and observance.
2. Freedom to manifest one's religion or beliefs shall be subject only to such limitations as are prescribed by law and are necessary in a democratic society in the interests of public safety, for the protection of public order, health or morals, or for the protection of the rights and freedoms of others.

Article 10

Freedom of expression
1. Everyone has the right to freedom of expression. This right shall include freedom to hold opinions and to receive and impart information and ideas without interference by public authority and regardless of frontiers. This Article shall not prevent states from requiring the licensing of broadcasting, television or cinema enterprises.
2. The exercise of these freedoms, since it carries with it duties and responsibilities, may be subject to such formalities, conditions, restrictions or penalties as are prescribed by law and are necessary in a democratic society, in the interests of national security, territorial integrity or public safety, for the prevention of disorder or crime, for the protection of health or morals, for the protection of the reputation or rights of others, for preventing the disclosure of information received in confidence, or for maintaining the authority and impartiality of the judiciary.

Article 11

Freedom of assembly and association

1. Everyone has the right to freedom of peaceful assembly and to freedom of association with others, including the right to form and to join trade unions for the protection of his interests.
2. No restrictions shall be placed on the exercise of these rights other than such as are prescribed by law and are necessary in a democratic society in the interests of national security or public safety, for the prevention of disorder or crime, for the protection of health or morals or for the protection of the rights and freedoms of others. This Article shall not prevent the imposition of lawful restrictions on the exercise of these rights by members of the armed forces, of the police or of the administration of the state.

Article 12

Right to marry

Men and women of marriageable age have the right to marry and to found a family, according to the national laws governing the exercise of this right.

Article 13

Right to an effective remedy

Everyone whose rights and freedoms as set forth in this Convention are violated shall have an effective remedy before a national authority notwithstanding that the violation has been committed by persons acting in an official capacity.

Article 14

Prohibition of discrimination

The enjoyment of the rights and freedoms set forth in this Convention shall be secured without discrimination on any ground such as sex, race, colour, language, religion, political or other opinion, national or social origin, association with a national minority, property, birth or other status.

Article 15

Derogation in time of emergency

1. In time of war or other public emergency threatening the life of the nation any High Contracting Party may take measures derogating from its obligations under this Convention to the extent strictly required by the exigencies of the situation, provided that such measures are not inconsistent with its other obligations under international law.

2. No derogation from Article 2, except in respect of deaths resulting from lawful acts of war, or from Articles 3, 4(paragraph 1) and 7 shall be made under this provision.

3. Any High Contracting Party availing itself of this right of derogation shall keep the Secretary General of the Council of Europe fully informed of the measures which it has taken and the reasons therefor. It shall also inform the Secretary General of the Council of Europe when such measures have ceased to operate and the provisions of the Convention are again being fully executed.

Article 16

Restrictions on political activity of aliens
Nothing in Articles 10, 11 and 14 shall be regarded as preventing the High Contracting Parties from imposing restrictions on the political activity of aliens.

Article 17

Prohibition of abuse of rights
Nothing in this Convention may be interpreted as implying for any state, group or person any right to engage in any activity or perform any act aimed at the destruction of any of the rights and freedoms set forth herein or at their limitation to a greater extent than is provided for in the Convention.

Article 18

Limitation on use of restrictions on rights
The restrictions permitted under this Convention to the said rights and freedoms shall not be applied for any purpose other than those for which they have been prescribed.

The first protocol

Article 1

Protection of property
Every natural or legal person is entitled to the peaceful enjoyment of his possessions. No one shall be deprived of his possessions except in the public interest and subject to the conditions provided for by law and by the general principles of international law. The preceding provisions shall not, however, in any way impair the right of a state to enforce such laws as it deems necessary to control the use of property in accordance with the general interest or to secure the payment of taxes or other contributions or penalties.

Article 2

Right to education
No person shall be denied the right to education. In the exercise of any functions which it assumes in relation to education and to teaching, the state shall respect the right of parents to ensure such education and teaching in conformity with their own religious and philosophical convictions.

Article 3

Right to free elections
The High Contracting Parties undertake to hold free elections at reasonable intervals by secret ballot, under conditions which will ensure the free expression of the opinion of the people in the choice of the legislature.

The sixth protocol

Article 1

Abolition of the death penalty
The death penalty shall be abolished. No one shall be condemned to such penalty or executed.

Article 2

Death penalty in time of war
A state may make provision in its law for the death penalty in respect of acts committed in time of war or of imminent threat of war; such penalty shall be applied only in the instances laid down in the law and in accordance with its provisions. The state shall communicate to the Secretary General of the Council of Europe the relevant provisions of that law.

Human rights instruments – disabled people

- UN (1966) International Covenant on Civil and Political Rights.
- UN (1966) International Covenant on Economic, Social and Cultural Rights.
- UN (1971) Declaration on the Rights of Mentally Retarded Persons.
- UN (1975) Declaration on the Rights of Disabled Persons.
- UN (1991) Principles for the Protection of Persons with Mental Illnesses and the Improvement of Mental Health Care.
- UN (1993) Standard Rules on the Equalization of Opportunities for Persons with Disabilities.
- UN (1994) General Comment No 5, Persons with Disabilities Committee on Economic, Social and Cultural Rights.
- UN (1994) Towards full integration of persons with disabilities in society: implementation of the Standard Rules on the Equalization of Opportunities for Persons with Disabilities, and of the Long-Term Strategy to Implement the World Programme of Action concerning Disabled Persons to the Year 2000 and Beyond.
- COE (1965) European Social Charter, (and revised 1999).
- COE (1992) Recommendation No R (92) 6 (Committee of Ministers) 9 April 1992 on a coherent policy for people with disabilities.
- COE (1990) Recommendation No R (90) 22 on the protection of the mental health of certain vulnerable groups in society.
- COE (1989) European Convention for the Prevention of Torture and Inhuman or Degrading Treatment or Punishment.
- COE (1999) European Convention for the Protection of Human Rights and Dignity of the Human Being with Regard to the Application of Biology and Medicine: Convention on Human Rights and Biomedicine.
- COE (2000) White Paper on the protection of the human rights and dignity of people suffering from mental disorder, especially those placed as involuntary patients in a psychiatric establishment.

These instruments can be accessed at various Internet addresses, although the University of Minnesota Human Rights Library has an excellent site at:
    www1.umn.edu/humanrts/index.html
For a comprehensive overview of the UN disability related provisions, see Quinn and Degener, 2000.

Useful Internet addresses

The 1988 Human Rights Act
The full text of the 1998 Human Rights Act and other UK legislation since 1988 can be found on the HMSO web site at:
www.legislation.hmso.gov.uk/acts.htm

European Court of Human Rights
Almost all the Court judgments and Commission decisions are accessible on the Council of Europe case research website at:
www.echr.coe.int/hudoc/

Other international Human Rights Covenants and so on
Details of these can be obtained from various sites, although the University of Minnesota Human Rights Centre has an excellent website at:
www1.umn.edu/humanrts/

General information on the 1998 Human Rights Act
The Lord Chancellor's office human rights website is to be found at:
www.lcd.gov.uk/hract/hramenu.htm

Court of Appeal decisions
Some decisions of the Court of Appeal can be accessed from the Court Service website at:
www.courtservice.gov.uk/

House of Lords judgments
All recent (post-1998 Human Rights Act) judgments of the House of Lords are available on the Internet at:
www.parliament.the-stationery-office.co.uk/pa/ld199697/ldjudgmt/ldjudgmt.htm

US Supreme Court judgments
US Supreme Court judgments can be accessed through various search engines, including:
www.findlaw.com/casecode/supreme.html

Index

T

terminology of legal profession xiv
thought, freedom of 24, 69-70, 116
Tickner, V. 91
torture 19, 22, 26
  see also degrading treatment
transsexuals 62
Treaty of Amsterdam xiv
tribunals 58
Tyne, A. 10

V

Valuing People (White Paper) 79n.13
victim support: lack of 3-4
voluntary sector 9, 10
voting rights 26, 71-2, 119

W

waiting lists 51-2
Warnock Report (1978) 10-11
welfare rights 6-7